FREEDOMBEGINSHERE

DevotionalJournal

Foreword by
DR.GARY**SMALLEY**

CONTENTS

 FOREWORD

"It is for freedom that Christ has set us free."
– Galatians 5:1

I can't begin to tell you how blessed I am to be a part of Freedom Begins Here. This is one of the most encouraging, hope filled programs I have ever seen. You will walk away from this program with renewed passion for life-change. You will be changed from the inside out if you simply open your heart to what God wants to do in your life. He wants you to be free! He wants you to walk in freedom.

From the very first time I read Dr. Mark Laaser's book, I knew God had inspired this man to give us a successful road map to overcome sexual sin. He has walked the path and now is leading men and women down the same path of freedom. Partnering with Dr. Laaser makes total sense for me and for the work I do with couples all around the world.

I am also thrilled to be hosting this program with my pastor and friend, Ted Cunningham. He has a heart for seeing men and women set free and seeing families restored. Clay and Renee Crosse will inspire you to make the decision to change. Their down to earth approach and gutsy vulnerability is contagious. I hope you catch that recovery from sexual sin is to be celebrated within the church.

The silence must end. We need people to see the church as a place of safety and recovery. That is my passion behind this project. I want the church to start talking about it. I want the church to help millions find Jesus. And I believe Freedom Begins Here is a catalyst in that worldwide revival.

If you are struggling or flirting with pornography or sexual sin, then I pray Freedom Begins Here will be a wake-up call for you, challenging you to guard your heart. If you are addicted, Freedom Begins Here is your first step. Watch every minute of the DVD program and read every word of this devotional. Cry out to God, who will supernaturally give you the power you need to find freedom.

If you are not struggling or addicted, but are participating in Freedom Begins Here on behalf of a loved one or friend, my prayer for you is that God will use you in the journey of the one needing to find freedom.

May God use Freedom Begins Here for his glory alone!

Blessings,
Dr. Gary Smalley

❧ INTRODUCTION

Author and speaker Josh McDowell tells audiences that the most important sexual organ is . . . the brain. How we think about life—past hurts and present hopes, the desire to control people or having respect for them, the compulsion to escape or the courage to face reality—determines our choices. That's what this devotional is about: identifying and replacing destructive patterns of thought, and learning to think in a way that is far more healthy and productive.

The apostle Paul understood that right thinking is the key to making good choices. In several of his letters, he encouraged people to focus their minds on good things. To the Philippians, he wrote about the powerful combination of right thinking and spending time with people who model godly decisions. He told them, "And now, dear brothers and sisters, one final thing. Fix your thoughts on what is true, and honorable, and right, and pure, and lovely, and admirable. Think about things that are excellent and worthy of praise. Keep putting into practice all you learned and received from me—everything you heard from me and saw me doing. Then the God of peace will be with you." (Philippians 4:8-9)

God's Gift

Sex is a gift from God—a good gift that brings fulfillment and draws people closer together if they engage in it according to his direction. Sexual expression in the purity of God's design is a source of tremendous joy and intimacy. Mankind, though, has almost limitless capacity to distort God's gifts. We turn food into eating disorders and obesity, we turn grapes and grain into alcoholism and we turn friendly competition into compulsive gambling. The greater the gift, the greater the evil in its distortion. Sex is one of God's greatest gifts and our misuse of it destroys lives—ours and everyone who is touched by our sexual sins.

Sexual sin isn't just a male problem. Studies show that one-third of sex addicts are women. However, not everyone who engages in sexual sin is addicted. Like most addictions, people often move through distinct stages: first, *experimenting* with porn sites or flirting with people they're not married to; then, *seeking* more exciting and riskier experiences that become habits. Gradually (or not so gradually), it takes more and more excitement to create the sense of release and pleasure and we start *obsessing* about having sexual thrills. When life is dominated by thoughts of sex, acting out and the consequences of these exploits, people become *sex addicts*.

You may have picked up this book because you find yourself thinking about things you never dreamed you'd let your mind dwell on and you want to arrest the slide toward addiction and destruction right now.

You may have picked it up because you have a secret life (or at least you hope it's secret) and you need help to climb out of the hole you're in.

You may have picked up this book because your life is consumed with sexual fantasies and acts and every aspect of your life—your family, your finances, your career and your friendships—is being destroyed by your addiction to sex.

Or perhaps you picked it up because you love someone who is struggling with sexual problems and you want to find a way to help.

Whatever the reason, you have made an important first step. Finding freedom from sexual sin isn't always easy, but it is well worth the effort.

Breeding Ground

Fantasies are the breeding ground for acting out sexually. Illusions of sexual exploits often combine real people with imaginary situations in our minds. These images stay in our memories for years and they can surface at the most unexpected moments and consume our attention. All who are involved in sexual sin play mind games to enflame desire, deny the problem, justify it, or minimize the severity. Christians, in whom the Holy Spirit communicates truth and conviction, struggle very hard to convince themselves that their sexual sin isn't really happening, or that they can't help it, or that it really isn't that bad. Dr. Mark Laaser, author of *Healing the Wounds of Sexual Addiction*, observes, "Fantasies are a messenger of the soul. The soul is basically trying to create an answer to the deepest desires of the heart."

A mind that dwells on sexual fantasies, often aided by pornography and masturbation, soon destroys the barriers that kept the person from sliding down the slippery slope into sexual misconduct. Before long, the unthinkable becomes possible, the possible enflames desire, desire creates a plan to act and these actions then seem totally logical.

In the mind of a person consumed by sex, the intense tension between shame and desire is played out day after day. In his book *Out of the Shadows*, Patrick Carnes identified "The Sexual Addiction Cycle" [see diagram on page 163]. Fantasizing leads to prescribed rituals (looking at online porn sites, going to a certain bar, putting on particular clothes, drinking or using drugs to lower inhibitions, etc.), which almost inevitably lead to acting out. The actions can be mild or extreme, committed alone or with others, in private or public. The rush of adrenaline and neurochemicals in the brain can be, quite literally, addictive, but after the event, the person comes down from the high and despair sets in. Sooner or later, thoughts of self-deprecation and shame lead the person to escape into fantasies and the cycle continues.

The Way Out

No matter who we are or what we've done, Jesus Christ offers us hope for a new life of joy, freedom and integrity. Like Jesus' story of the prodigal son who squandered everything by "wild living," our sexual choices may have hurt the ones we love and ruined our reputations, but we can turn toward home to find a loving, forgiving Father. God's forgiveness, however, didn't come cheap. Our sins deserve punishment, and Jesus took our punishment for us. When we grasp the enormity of his love—it's big enough that God sent his son to die to pay for our despicable, shameful sins—gratitude overwhelms us.

The way out of sexual sins involves turning to God and finding a friend or a group to help us. We may have tried to keep our sexual sins a secret, but the healing process necessarily involves connecting with a sponsor, group, pastor, or counselor who will speak truth to us, encourage us when we're faltering, and kick us in the seat of our pants when we need some tough love.

The journey into sexual sin probably took some time as we moved through experimentation to our current behaviors and the path to emotional healing, spiritual strength and sexual purity takes many steps, too. The road is sometimes smooth, but it's occasionally steep and rocky. Times of exhilarating insight and hope can be punctuated by discouragement, but the struggle to keep going is worth it. Countless men and women have traveled this road with trusted friends as guides and they've found God's love and strength all along the way.

What can you expect as you work through this devotional and take steps toward wholeness? Most of us experience a strange mix of resistance and hope. We long for freedom and forgiveness, but somehow, the pattern we've developed is familiar . . . comforting . . . and less threatening than change, even healthy, positive change. Our thinking processes drift back to the old patterns of fantasy and rituals and the old attractions of people, places and things call our name and invite us to come back. They promise to make us feel good again and if we're not careful, we'll believe them.

People have many motivations for recovery from patterns of sexual sin and addiction. For some, the legal system has caught them breaking the law and they can't avoid reality any longer, because now it's headline news. Others realize they've ruined (or are ruining) their most cherished relationships and they're willing to do whatever it takes to restore them. Some people have thoughts of suicide and if they don't get help soon, it may all be over. And some refuse to continue for another day to live a secret life full of lies; they're ready for a new beginning. For all of these people, a sense of desperation is the key to change. With it, high walls can be climbed, but without it, we stay stuck in our hopelessness, helplessness and selfishness.

Make no mistake: The road to recovery from patterns of sexual sin can be difficult. Our greatest struggles, however, result in a deeper appreciation of God's grace, love, and power—and that's not a bad result from a difficult road trip.

Take this Test

The "Sexual Addiction Screening Test" was developed by Patrick Carnes to help people determine the presence and level of sexual addiction. Many people have found it helpful in assessing their level of emotional pain, sexual lusts and misconduct. Answer "yes" or "no" for each one and add up your "yes" answers.

1. Were you sexually abused as a child or adolescent?

Yes   No

2. Do you regularly purchase romance novels or sexually explicit magazines?

Yes   No

3. Have you stayed in romantic relationships after they have become emotionally or physically abusive?

Yes   No

4. Do you often find yourself preoccupied with sexual thoughts or romantic daydreams?

Yes   No

5. Do you feel that your sexual behavior is not normal?

Yes   No

6. Does your spouse (or significant other(s)) ever worry or complain about your sexual behavior?

Yes   No

7. Do you have trouble stopping your sexual behavior when you know it is inappropriate?

Yes   No

8. Do you ever feel bad about your sexual behavior?

Yes   No

9. Has your sexual behavior ever created problems for you and your family?

Yes   No

10. Have you ever sought help for sexual behavior you did not like?

Yes   No

11. Have you ever worried about people finding out about your sexual activities?

Yes   No

12. Has anyone been hurt emotionally because of your sexual behavior?

Yes   No

13. Have you ever participated in sexual activity in exchange for money or gifts?

Yes   No

14. Do you have times when you act out sexually followed by periods of celibacy (no sex at all)?

Yes   No

15. Have you made efforts to quit a type of sexual activity and failed?

Yes   No

16. Do you hide some of your sexual behavior from others?

Yes   No

17. Do you find yourself having multiple romantic relationships at the same time?

Yes   No

18. Have you ever felt degraded by your sexual behavior?

Yes   No

19. Has sex or romantic fantasies been a way for you to escape your problems?

Yes   No

20. When you have sex, do you feel depressed afterwards?

Yes   No

21. Do you regularly engage in sadomasochistic behavior?

Yes   No

22. Has your sexual activity interfered with your family life?

Yes   No

23. Have you had sexual activity with minors?

Yes   No

24. Do you feel controlled by your sexual desire or fantasies of romance?

Yes   No

25. Do you ever think your sexual desire is stronger than you are?

Yes   No

Add up your responses: _____ Yes   _____ No

A score of 1—3 in the "yes" column indicates a possible area of concern and should be openly discussed with a friend or family member.

More than 3 "yes" answers may indicate the need to consider professional counseling and joining a support group.

A score of 6 or more clearly presents a problem with potentially self-abusive and/or dangerous consequences. Seek professional help as soon as possible.

What did you learn about yourself by taking this test? An accurate assessment is the foundation for taking bold steps of change.

OK, now you're ready to begin a 30-day journey of renewing your mind. The goal isn't to check off a box that you've read the devotional for the day. Instead, the goal is to let God's Spirit work deeply in your heart to impart truth and grace to you. Before you begin each day's study, ask God to give you insight and the courage to act on what you learn. As you read and answer the questions, take an extra moment to let the truth sink in and allow the Holy Spirit to nudge you toward honesty and integrity. Some days will be very encouraging and some will challenge you to the depths of your soul. All of them are designed to retrain and renew your mind so that your life reflects more of the goodness and greatness of God.

In the first week, find someone (a mature friend, pastor, counselor or sponsor in a support group) who will walk this journey with you. You may have felt trapped in your lifestyle—and you may still feel that way now—but in these 30 days, you'll realize that you have choices every minute of every day to focus your thoughts on what is good and right and wholesome, or to let your mind drift back into the swamp of sexual sin. To reinforce what you're learning on this journey, make it a habit to listen to good Christian music and download talks by inspiring Christian leaders and teachers. With a little effort, you can find a universe of great stuff to fill your thoughts! Make the effort. Your family, your friends, your God and sooner or later you, too, will be delighted you did.

BERNIE'S STORY

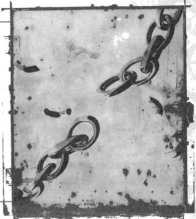

"You've got to give up the secret. Pornography loses its grip, it loses its power..."

You arrive at a point where you have to say, "I don't care what it takes, I don't care how painful it will be. I am going let God do this work to restore me and to bring me back to real life. Because the life that I'm living now isn't the life that I was meant to live and this is a hell that I cannot live through any longer."

You've got to give up the secret. Pornography loses its grip, it loses its power when you begin to realize that you are loved and you are significant beyond what pornography has to offer. And that, no matter what you do, you won't be rejected by God.

Bernie

Excerpt from the DVD Freedom Begins Here: Personal Toolkit. View this and other personal stories in their entirety in the special features portion of this DVD release. Available at many Christian Booksellers or online at www.freedombeginshere.org

DAY 1

NO MATTER WHAT YOU'VE DONE

"So he returned home to his father. And while he was still a long way off, his father saw him coming. Filled with love and compassion, he ran to his son, embraced him, and kissed him."

– Luke 15:20

This guy had really blown it! In this story of a son who turned his back on his father, Jesus made his point crystal-clear. He described the young man's greed to have his inheritance—before his father had died. As soon as he got his hands on the cash, he headed off to a distant country, where he wasted it all on "wild living." When he found himself suddenly penniless and friendless, he got a job on a farm feeding slop to pigs. He was so hungry that he wanted to eat the nasty mess they were eating. The Jews considered pigs to be untouchable, but this young man's job was feeding pigs.

In our culture, it's hard for us to grasp the horror that must have crossed people's faces as they listened to Jesus tell this story. To the Jewish people, nothing could have been more despicable, more shameful, more degrading than for a person to dishonor his father by selfish greed and then stooping to feed pigs!

After a while, the young man "came to his senses" and realized that his father's servants had a far better life than he had, so he headed for home. On the way home, he carefully rehearsed his apology to his father. Since he had abdicated his role as a son, he planned to ask to become a servant on his father's land. When he was approaching the house from far down the road, he looked up and saw someone running toward him. The figure in the distance grew larger and soon he realized it was his father. He had expected to be greeted coolly, but he sure didn't expect his dad to run toward him!

We can only imagine the scene as the shame-filled young man's father got closer. Instead of angrily condemning his son, his father gave him the biggest hug of his life and kissed him! His dad called out to his servants to bring the best robe for his son and the ring that signified full acceptance back into the family and he started preparations for the biggest party of their lives.

For two millennia, this story has thrilled and amazed us. It communicates the most powerful message of forgiveness and love—God's forgiveness and love for all of us who have squandered our lives in wild living, bad choices, and selfish actions. The father didn't excuse the son. He forgave him. He didn't make the son jump through hoops to earn his love. He loved him unconditionally, warmly and totally.

Does it seem too good to be true? Have you done things that are so selfish and sinful that you can't imagine God forgiving you and calling you his dear child? Then this message is for you; it is for all of us. God is not scowling at us because we've sinned. He's been waiting . . . longing for us to come back, watching down the road to see when we'll appear and he's ready to shower his forgiveness and love on any who return with a broken heart.

DAY1 REFLECTION

Imagine yourself as the young man. Describe the shame you'd feel in the pigpen and the wonder of your father forgiving you, hugging you, kissing you and celebrating your return.

_____

_____

What did the son do to be reinstated? What did the father do?

_____

_____

DAY1 PRAYER

Dear Father, thank you so much for loving me, forgiving me, restoring me as your child and celebrating my return. Today, I accept your forgiveness for:

_____

_____

FREEDOMBEGINS**HERE**

 # DAY**2**

FACE TO FACE

"In one of the villages, Jesus met a man with an advanced case of leprosy. When the man saw Jesus, he bowed with his face to the ground, begging to be healed. 'Lord,' he said, 'if you are willing, you can heal me and make me clean.' Jesus reached out and touched him. 'I am willing,' he said. 'Be healed!' And instantly the leprosy disappeared."

– Luke 5:12-13

For months, years and even decades, we've tried to hide our shame. We felt terrible about our insatiable sexual desires and our secret, sordid acts, but we've avoided the painful truth about our behavior at all costs. We justified it ("I needed it"), we excused it ("I couldn't help it"), we minimized it ("It wasn't that bad") and we denied it ("Not me, I don't have a problem").

Luke's story of the life of Christ contains many encounters of men and women who came face to face with Christ after they came face to face with their desperate need for him. A woman had been hemorrhaging for 12 years, but she reached out to touch Jesus' cloak as he walked by. Zacchaeus was a despised tax collector who had extorted money from his neighbors, but he climbed a tree to see the man who could forgive any sin. A prostitute was so touched by her encounter with Christ that she barged into the home of a religious leader to express her gratitude to Jesus. And a leper, an object of taunts and extreme rejection, fell at Jesus' feet and proclaimed his faith that Jesus could heal him.

For men and women shamed by their lack of ability to control their sexual desires, the leper offers a wonderful example of honesty, hope and healing. If this man had been like many of us who are stuck in denial, he might have gotten up that morning, looked in the mirror and said to himself, "You know, my nose has rotted off and my ears are missing, but I'm looking pretty sharp today! In fact, I don't have any problems at all. Sure, I live in a cesspool with others like me, but we're having a great time together."

On this day, though, he offered no excuses, no rationalization, and no sugarcoating of the cold, hard truth. Perhaps there were hundreds of other lepers there that day, but this man had the courage to be honest about his desperate need, and he came out of the crowd and fell at Jesus' feet to ask for help. With deep humility, he didn't demand anything. He only spoke the truth that Jesus could heal him if he was willing. And yes, Jesus was willing. In fact, in a moment that horrified everyone around them, Jesus reached out and touched the leper's putrid flesh. Has there ever been a more grace-filled moment?

And it all started when a man looked in the mirror, recognized the rotten, stinking condition of his life and mustered enough courage to see Jesus face to face to express his need.

DAY**2** REFLECTION

Describe the powerful mixture of fear and hope that might have been in the leper's heart the moment before he fell at Jesus' feet.

_____

_____

Are you ready to come face to face with Jesus? Why or why not?

_____

_____

DAY**2** PRAYER

Lord Jesus, I see the rotten mess in my life and I fall at your feet to ask for your touch and your cleansing. Thank you for being willing to touch this part of me:

_____

_____

# DAY**3**

TO TELL THE TRUTH

"If we claim we have no sin, we are only fooling ourselves and not living in the truth. But if we confess our sins to him, he is faithful and just to forgive us our sins and to cleanse us from all wickedness."

– 1 John 1:8-9

Years ago, a bearded man dressed in a robe showed up outside a church service in Chapel Hill, N.C., claiming to have the power to heal people suffering from any disease. For hours, he tried to convince people that he had this ability, but then someone challenged him: "The hospital isn't far away. Let's go over there so we can watch you heal all the patients."

The man led the procession to the hospital and they rode elevators to a floor with many cancer patients. With appropriate dramatic effect, he held out his hands and solemnly asked God to heal people. Nothing happened.

People want to find someone who can authentically forgive sins and heal wounds. Our search can lead us in all kinds of directions to listen to strange people make glowing promises, but only One has the authority to promise forgiveness and deliver on his promise: Jesus Christ. Why do you think so many people flocked to him? Thousands crowded onto hillsides to hear him and many others followed his every move to watch him heal, forgive and transform those he touched. In a hilarious account, four men tried to carry their paralytic friend to be healed by Jesus. The house where Jesus was speaking was so crowded that the men couldn't get in, so they climbed onto the roof and knocked a hole in it to lower their buddy in front of Jesus. We can just imagine the smile on Jesus' face as he heard clawing and hammering on the roof above him. Pieces of plaster fell all around him and suddenly a man on a stretcher came down on ropes! He must have loved seeing their faith. These men and all the others Jesus touched, believed that Jesus' promises were good and true.

In the opening paragraph of John's first letter, he reminds us that Jesus' promise to forgive is still valid and will remain valid for people who are honest enough to admit their sins to him. Denial won't cut it, but we probably won't be honest unless we have genuine hope that our honesty will be rewarded with the wonderful cleansing that comes from Christ's forgiveness.

John and Jesus don't want any of us to be confused. The promise of forgiveness is valid because Jesus has already paid the price to forgive us. When we "confess our sins to him," we agree that the attitudes and behaviors the Spirit has pointed out as sin are, indeed, sin. Our sins deserve punishment, and we also agree that

Jesus' death is the substitute for the death our sins deserve. When we agree with God, the forgiveness Jesus paid for on the cross becomes real in our experience.

We may not want to tell the truth to another person because we aren't sure that person will forgive us, but we can be completely confident that Jesus forgives us and washes us clean from the filth in our lives. That's his promise and we can count on it.

DAY3 REFLECTION

Have you resisted telling the truth to Jesus about your sins because you weren't sure you'd be forgiven? Explain.

_____

_____

What would it mean to you to trust this promise of forgiveness? How would it affect your walk with God, your relationships and your desire to live a clean life?

_____

_____

# DAY**3** PRAYER

Jesus, story after story in Scripture and promise after promise tell me that you will do what you say you'll do. Right now, I want to tell you the things I've done that displease you.

_____

_____

I agree with you that those things are sin. Thank you so much that you've paid for each one of them on the cross so I can be forgiven!

 # DAY**4**

RUBBING OFF

"Walk with the wise and become wise;

associate with fools and get in trouble."

– Proverbs 13:20

It ain't rocket science. In fact, it's one of the most predictable and simple principles in life: we become like the people we hang out with. Sexual sin, ranging from occasional misbehavior to obsessive addiction, includes private and public elements. We may engage in private fantasies, masturbation and pornography, but we also spend time with people who tell dirty jokes, invite us to go to strip clubs, help us find prostitutes and happily relate story after story of sexual exploits. In these relationships, acceptance is based on two things: keeping secrets and affirming each other's sexual desires and behavior. We make fun of people who are straight and clean. "They just don't get it," we snicker to each other. And we avoid people who live clean, upright, noble lives because they make us feel uncomfortable.

Just look where these "friends" have gotten us. We're always looking over our shoulder to see if our spouse, children, friends and co-workers are on our trail and might discover our secrets.

We live two parallel lives, one thoroughly sexualized with fantasies and secret acting-out, and the other looking like we belong on the front pew in church. We drift toward the people who "understand" our dilemma and assure us that we're only doing what comes naturally.

But we've been fools, and they've led us into more trouble than we ever dreamed possible. The way out of sexual sin doesn't just happen. We need rigorous honesty and we need a true friend to listen, point us in a good direction and celebrate every step of restoration. You don't know people like that? Yes, you do, you just haven't valued them.

Every grieving soul knows that finding a wise friend is essential to our process of taking steps forward. You probably already know someone who has been in recovery from alcohol, drugs, gambling or food addictions. This person may not have sexual problems, but he or she understands the process of recovery and can be a valuable ally. Perhaps a counselor or a pastor will be the person who listens as you tell your story and helps you rebuild your life, and if you get into a support group, your sponsor will help you every step along the way.

The proverb is crystal-clear and millions of people can attest to its truth: when we spend time with wise people, their wisdom rubs off on us, but when we hang out with fools, we get into big trouble.

Each of us has a choice. Change is hard, but finding a wise friend is one of the most important choices we can make as we make strides to refresh our minds, renew our souls, and restore relationships with those we love.

DAY**4** REFLECTION

How has spending time with fools caused trouble in your life? Describe how their attitudes and words have reinforced your bad choices.

_____

_____

Who is one wise person who can help you?

_____

_____

DAY**4** PRAYER

Father, I've valued the wrong people. I've thought fools were cool and I've believed them far too much. This has to change. Lead me to a wise person who can help me. That person might be_____.

 # DAY**5**

LIKE CHANGING CLOTHES

"...throw off your old sinful nature and your former way of life, which is corrupted by lust and deception. Instead, let the Spirit renew your thoughts and attitudes. Put on your new nature, created to be like God—truly righteous and holy."

– Ephesians 4:22-24

Some people claim the Christian life is "effortless." They tell people that following Christ is "getting caught up in the jet stream of the Spirit and carried along." Wow! That sounds pretty good, but it's not the whole story. Sure, we can take a verse or two out of context and make them sound like the Christian life is a breeze and that change is really easy because God does it all for us, but even a casual reading of Scripture gives us a very different picture.

Virtually every person described in the Bible had choices to make, hard choices that tested their faith and challenged their courage. The listing of men and women in Hebrews 11, the "Hall of Faith," includes people who struggled to know God and follow his will. They made this list not because they found it easy, but because they kept trusting God even when following him was difficult.

Paul understood the tension between the work of God's Spirit and our responsibility to make good choices. Both are at work; both are essential. In his letter to the Ephesians, he compared our choices to changing clothes: we "throw off" the old and "put on" the new. When we change clothes, we don't just stand in the dressing room while our clothes magically come off and end up in the hamper. We pay attention to each button, each snap, each lace and each piece of clothing. And we make a decision to take each one off. In the same way, we look at our lives and see examples of our old way of life. We grab our sinful behaviors and attitudes and we throw them away by saying "no" to them. But nature, as the physicists say, abhors a vacuum. If we don't replace bad habits with good ones, they'll come back in a heartbeat. We have to also choose to "put on" thinking about good things, doing noble things and spending time with people who pursue God.

What does that look like? Every sinful, selfish action has to be identified as destructive and replaced with something good. For instance, if your ritual is to go into the den to look at online porn after everybody in the family has gone to bed, make a point of going to bed when your spouse does or go to another room in the house to listen to Christian music or to read an uplifting book. Make the choices. That's what Paul is saying. Change begins with our thoughts. We "let the Spirit renew [our] thoughts and attitudes" as we read Scripture, listen to messages that encourage faith and purity and interact with friends who love Christ. God's Spirit wants to engage our minds and hearts. All we need to do, as a man once said, is "give God a chance!" We have a hundred choices about our thought life every day. We can choose to drift back into fantasies that lead to acting out, or we can choose to latch our minds on to ideas and truths that are true, right, noble and pure.

The Christian life isn't easy, but we can make genuine progress as we make choices every day to "throw away" selfish behaviors and "put on" healthy ones, while we fill our minds with ideas about God's love and his purposes for us. It's like changing clothes.

DAY5 REFLECTION

What are some things you need to "throw off"?

_____

_____

What are some specific attitudes and behaviors you need to "put on" to replace the things you are throwing off?

_____

_____

Make a list of books, online talks, uplifting music and other re-sources you can use to renew your mind. (If you don't know, where can you look first?)

_____

_____

☃ DAY**5** PRAYER

Dear Father, choices about change have seemed overwhelm-ing to me, so I haven't even tried, or I've tried a lot of times and quit. Today, I understand that change comes in small deci-sions. I am right now making a decision to "throw off": _____ _____ and "put on": _____ _____. And I will fill my mind with _____

OMAR'S STORY

"Just living free from addiction is not having an abundant life – that's survival."

Having an abundant life is to be happy and joyful. To be able to share your testimony with people. That's abundant life. That's a life of freedom and joy, not just saying, "Well, it's just another day when I can't look at pornography cause God doesn't want me to."

Just living free from addiction is not having an abundant life – that's survival.

Omar

Excerpt from the DVD <u>Freedom Begins Here: Personal Toolkit</u>. View this and other personal stories in their entirety in the special features portion of this DVD release. Available at many Christian Booksellers or online at www.freedombeginshere.org

DAY**6**

EVEN ME?

"This is a trustworthy saying, and everyone should accept it: 'Christ Jesus came into the world to save sinners'—and I am the worst of them all. But God had mercy on me so that Christ Jesus could use me as a prime example of his great patience with even the worst sinners."

– 1 Timothy 1:15-16

People who struggle with addictions and secret behaviors often echo the person who said dejectedly, "Yeah, God might work in other people's lives, but not in mine. I think it's hopeless."

No one is beyond the grace of God. In fact, the most revered people in the Bible were flawed—deeply flawed. We think of Abraham as the father of our faith, but early in his walk with God, he was a coward who twice told kings that his beautiful wife was his sister so they wouldn't kill him and take her. If she was his sister, he surmised, they could take her without killing him!

We know Moses as the great man of God who led the people of Israel out of slavery in Egypt and met God face to face. Earlier, though, Moses killed a man in an outburst of rage and buried the body to hide his crime, and later, when God tapped Moses on the shoulder to give him the role of leading his people, Moses came up with a lame excuse that he couldn't talk well enough—a murderer who became too timid.

David was known for his heart for God and his military victories. He was a fantastic leader, but one year, the army went out to battle while he stayed home. With time to kill and normal libido, he saw a beautiful woman taking a bath, and called her in to have sex with him. When he learned that she was pregnant, this "man of God" conspired to have her husband killed.

Paul wrote many letters in the New Testament and was the most influential believer in the history of the Christian faith, but before Christ touched him on the road to Damascus, Paul spent his time capturing and killing Christians! In his letter to Timothy, he didn't gloss over his sins. As he reflected on them, he concluded that he was "the worst of them all." But Paul didn't grovel in self-pity for being such a terrible person. He embraced the forgiveness and grace of Christ, and it made all the difference in his life.

It makes all the difference in our lives, too.

The free gift of God's forgiveness is broadcast in digital clarity. Many of us gladly embrace it, but some of us don't. Why? Why are some of us reluctant to accept God's grace the way Abraham, Moses, David, and Paul did? Because it's easier to complain than to change. We grumble and moan that God has abandoned us, or that he's working in another person's life, but not in ours. Hogwash. That's just an excuse to remain a coward stuck in the past instead of taking the risk to grab on to God's extended hand of goodness, greatness, and grace.

The grace of God is ready and available for you. Even you.

DAY**6** REFLECTION

As you read today's message, did your heart soar with expectancy of experiencing God's grace, or did you sense resistance in your soul? Explain.

_____

_____

What's the risk of embracing God's grace? What's the risk of not embracing it?

_____

_____

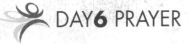 # DAY**6** PRAYER

Dear God, even me. I feel like I've been a murderer, a coward and a thief. Help me overcome my resistance. I reach out to you right now and accept your incredible grace. I may be the worst of sinners, but you are the best of forgivers. Thank you for:

_____

_____

DAY**7**

FREEDOM

"For the Lord is the Spirit, and wherever the Spirit of the Lord is, there is freedom."

– 2 Corinthians 3:17

"I've tried everything I know," he confided to a friend, "but I can't shake it. When I'm at work, I think about sex. When I'm at home, I think about getting away to a club so I can find a girl to have sex. When I'm having sex, I think of what I can do to get that person to meet me again tomorrow night. And in between, I hate myself for being such a terrible husband and father."

A woman wept as she told her story: "I had sex the first time when I was 14. It felt wonderful and awful at the same time. For some reason, I couldn't get enough, and by the time I was in college, I was roaming bars for pickups. I had sex with two or three men a night. Most of the time, I didn't even know their names." She sighed, "It's the only life I've known since I was a little girl. It feels like a prison and I can't find a way to escape."

The chemicals released by the brain make sexual sin one of the most addictive things known to medical science. It feels like a prison because it is a prison of the mind. Lying becomes a lifestyle, and in reality, all of the rituals around the acting-out become a way of life that seems right, normal and routine.

Freedom, though, is available for anyone who has a mustard seed of faith and enough courage to take the next step. We don't need the biggest faith in the world, just enough to invite Christ to touch the stinking, leprous skin of our shame. And we don't need to be as bold as lions with all the confidence in the world—we just need enough boldness to punch in the phone number of our sponsor or friend when we feel that we're going to fall again.

Christ's forgiveness flings the prison door open wide, but we find ourselves huddled in the darkness in the back of the cell, terrified to come out and terrified to stay. A kind voice invites us to come out, and we see a hand extended to us. As we step out into the light, we realize we're in worse shape than we ever imagined, but now we're holding someone's hand and we take another step into freedom.

Gradually, we gain strength and perspective. We begin to enjoy our freedom, and the more we realize how great it is, the more we're sure we never want to go back there again. But we haven't stopped being human. Freedom from the prison of sexual sin doesn't mean we aren't tempted. Yes, temptations come, but now we have the insight to see them for what they are: destruction waiting to happen! And instead of listening to the voices of fools who glory in their shame, we now listen to the voices of men and women who have gone through the same struggles and now know how to give and receive love instead of settling for a poor counterfeit.

This kind of freedom is a gift from God. We can't manufacture it, but we can treasure it and commit ourselves to honor Christ, the One who bought it for us. God's freedom isn't mindless escape. It's full of hope, purpose, truth and strength to know and follow Christ. Instead of hiding from God, we delight to live all day, every day in his presence, because where he is, there's freedom. God sets us free from the prison of our sexual sin, but we must dedicate ourselves more than ever to live in a way that matters.

Are you experiencing this freedom? Do you want to?

DAY**7** REFLECTION

Describe your experience in the prison of sexual sin.

_____

_____

What would it (or does it) look like for you to experience the freedom that only God can give?

_____

_____

 # DAY**7** PRAYER

Oh God, I want to be free! I want to wake up every day and not be consumed with sexual thoughts and actions. Thank you for paying the price for my release. I now take your hand and step out of the cell. Today, help me walk in freedom as I :

_____

_____

# DAY**8**

REACHING OUT

"A woman in the crowd had suffered for twelve years with constant bleeding, and she could find no cure. Coming up behind Jesus, she touched the fringe of his robe. Immediately, the bleeding stopped. . . . When the woman realized that she could not stay hidden, she began to tremble and fell to her knees in front of him. The whole crowd heard her explain why she had touched him and that she had been immediately healed. 'Daughter,' he said to her, 'your faith has made you well. Go in peace.'"

– Luke 8:43-44, 47-48

Jesus doesn't demand that we express perfect faith before he responds. All he asks is that we reach out with as much faith as we have at the time. This woman was at the end of her rope. She had been bleeding internally for 12 long years. By this time, she had spent all of her money on doctors, but they hadn't helped her. In that culture, sickness was thought to be a moral problem, so people in her community considered her an outcast. She had heard about an itinerant preacher who healed people—people just like her! She looked for him, but when she found him, he was surrounded by a mob of people. He was walking away, and maybe going with him was her last chance for healing and hope. She didn't have enough confidence or courage to stand in front of him and ask for help. As he walked by, she got down on the ground and reached through people's legs to touch the fringe of his robe.

Suddenly, everything changed. She felt a surge in her body, then she felt new again! At that moment, the crowd began to part and Jesus stood looking at her. She fell to the ground and explained what she'd done—as if he didn't already know. His smile told her that he was safe and she sensed his deep compassion for her. They talked for a while, and then Jesus turned to follow a man whose daughter had just died so he could touch her, too.

Don't miss what happened: Jesus isn't a bored, dispassionate salesman dispensing products for his customers. His goal wasn't just to heal this woman. He wanted to begin a relationship with her. He cared so much that he stopped along an urgent mission so he could connect with her, make eye contact with her and talk with her about her life.

The God of the universe is powerful enough to transform lives in a heartbeat and never break a sweat, but his goal is to relate to us. "I will be your God and you will be my people," he said to Abraham and other prophets in the Old Testament. And Jesus told his disciples, "I no longer call you servants but friends."

Friends. Just imagine. . . Almighty God wants us as his friends. No, he doesn't need us. We may become friends with someone because they meet a need or make us laugh, but God chose us as his friends in spite of our flaws.

What does it mean to have a friend like this? Our hearts burst with amazement that someone that powerful and loving would want to know us and spend time with us, and we realize that we have a lot to live up to. We don't want to do anything that will make him frown or tarnish his good name. No, what we do matters, and we want to honor him.

What does being God's friend mean to you?

 DAY**8** REFLECTION

How do you think the woman felt when Jesus stopped to connect with her?

_____

_____

How do you feel when you realize that God calls you his friend?

_____

_____

DAY**8** PRAYER

Dear Lord, I feel like the woman, with only a tiny faith that you'll do something wonderful in my life. The idea that you want to be my friend is mind-boggling to me. To me, being your friend means

_____

_____

 # DAY**9**

NO SHAME

"I am not sorry that I sent that severe letter to you . . . because the pain caused you to repent and change your ways. It was the kind of sorrow God wants his people to have, so you were not harmed by us in any way. For the kind of sorrow God wants us to experience leads us away from sin and results in salvation. There's no regret for that kind of sorrow. But worldly sorrow, which lacks repentance, results in spiritual death."

– 2 Corinthians 7:8-10

One of the biggest problems for people engaged in sexual sin is shame, but feelings of shame aren't always a bad thing. When we deny the reality of our sins, excuse our behavior and justify all the time we spend fantasizing about sex, we avoid feeling ashamed. In this case, the problem is that we don't feel appropriate shame for what we've done. If people say, "You should be ashamed," they're right! After we've repented, however, unwarranted shame can lock us into self-pity and passivity. That's quite a different problem. Before we repent, we desperately need God to shine his light on the ugliness and darkness of our hearts. When we grasp even a hint of how our sin offends God, ruins his image in us and harms others, we will feel terrible about what we've done and we'll cry out, "God, have mercy on me, a sinner!" A heartfelt, repentant response to shame is good and right and appropriate.

Repentance, though, brings cleansing. The believers in Corinth had done some shameful things, including degrading sexual sins that were considered bizarre, even in a sex-saturated city like Corinth. In a previous letter, Paul read them the riot act! In no uncertain terms, he told them that their behavior was abhorrent and that they needed to change—now! Later, he received a report that those he had reprimanded had, in fact, been appropriately ashamed, and they repented. In this letter, Paul explains that his severe language was entirely appropriate because it fit the depth of their sins. God's goal, though, is not just to blast people. He wants to produce godly sorrow, the kind of shame that produces repentance, change and, ultimately, hope.

Paul describes two kinds of sorrow (or shame). One produces death; the other produces life. The kind that results in death is the nagging, foreboding, oppressive sense that forgiveness is impossible. We've either done something "bad enough" or done it "long enough" to take us beyond the possibility of God's cleansing love. We've broken through denial about our sins, but instead of experiencing God's forgiveness, we're haunted by our sins all day, every day. The specter of past sins screams, "I'm a terrible person!" That kind of shame convinces us that God's love and power may be active for other people, but that he has abandoned us, leaving us hopeless, helpless, and feeling worthless. This kind of shame isn't from God.

Godly sorrow may begin with the same realization that we've greatly disappointed our loving God and Savior, but it embraces the forgiveness earned on the cross and is grateful—more grateful than ever before—for God's kindness to love us and his offer to cleanse us.

Feeling bad about what we've done is entirely appropriate when God's Spirit pricks our consciences and makes us painfully aware of the gravity of our sins. Godly sorrow, though, points us to Jesus so we can accept his forgiveness. At that point, morbid introspection, analyzing every word and action to try to find more sin to confess, isn't God's plan. In fact, that's the devil's doing. Fight it. Let godly sorrow have its way in you. Turn to God and thank him for his grace.

DAY9 REFLECTION

What are some differences between "godly sorrow" (the shame that leads to repentance and forgiveness) and "worldly sorrow" (the shame that results in hopelessness and passivity)?

_____

_____

Do you agree or disagree with the statement, "Many sinners use shame as a copout so they don't have to change?" Explain.

_____

_____

DAY**9** PRAYER

Dear Lord, you have shown me at least a little of the depth of my sin, and I'm horrified. God, have mercy on me, a sinner! I want to fully embrace your forgiveness so that "godly sorrow" will have a positive impact on my life. Now, when I feel ashamed, I will think about:

_____

_____

 DAY **10**

GOD'S PART AND OUR PART

"Work hard to show the results of your salvation, obeying God with deep reverence and fear. For God is working in you, giving you the desire and the power to do what pleases him."

— Philippians 2:12-13

Wounded people, addicted people and others with deep needs can get off balance in their view of the Christian life. The hill of strength and stability seems so hard to climb that they give up at the beginning and say, "Lord, I can't do anything. You have to do it all." That statement sounds noble and spiritual, but it isn't what the Bible says about the vast majority of instances in our lives. To be sure, there are times when we've tried everything we know to do, and we finally give up on self-effort to trust God. But many of us haven't tried hard at all. We've given up before we ever lifted a finger, and we wonder why we aren't making better progress.

To make sure we get his point, Paul tells us first about our part and then about God's part. First, he tells us to "work hard" to do the right thing. Our motivation is our gratitude for God's grace and we want to please the One who is both great and good. He deserves our very best efforts! But we aren't on our own. The next verse explains that even our desire to please God, the wisdom to make good decisions and the results of our efforts to do these things are all products of God's work in our lives. Our hard work and God's work in us—both, not one or the other.

In the process of overcoming sexual sin, many people pray, "Oh God, take this desire away from me," or "Lord, don't let me think this way anymore," or "God, keep me from sinning again." Quite often, though, they keep sinning over and over again, but after they've been praying this way for a while, they are angry with God for not coming through and answering their prayer. They miss the point: God is present and powerful, but he wants us to do our part. Our role is to make decisions and take action. Yes, these decisions have to be made when everything inside us screams for us to pursue our selfish sexual acts again, but it's up to us to make the right choices. We choose to fill our minds with Scripture, songs, talks, stories or anything else besides sexual fantasies. We choose to drive home from work on a road without a strip joint or an adult movie store. We get caller ID on our phone so we can refuse to take calls from people who don't support our new way of life. We turn off the computer at 9 p.m. We go home and play with the kids and talk with our spouse. We delete chat rooms and porn sites from our favorites list. In short, we do whatever it takes to move forward in our new, healthy, honorable lifestyle.

Choices like these take a lot of courage. It's easier to say, "I can't do it," and ask God to do it all for us, but that's not the way life works. God is waiting for us to take a step to do our part. When we take action, his Spirit moves to affirm, encourage and guide. Don't be misled: As we do our part, life doesn't necessarily become easier. In fact, it often becomes even harder at first because we have to take responsibility for the bad choices we've made. But God is with us, cheering us on and supporting us along the way. If things aren't working, we can be sure it's not because God isn't doing his part.

DAY 10 REFLECTION

What's the lure of passivity? Why does it feel better than taking responsibility and action?

_____

_____

In your growth and change right now, what is your part and what is God's part?

_____

_____

DAY 10 PRAYER

Dear Father, forgive me for blaming you that I haven't changed. I realize that I have to do my part and I know you'll do yours. Today, my part is:

_____

_____

CONNIE'S STORY

"...it is never one dimensional. It's never just about pornography..."

The thing that you have to understand about sexual addiction is that it is never one dimensional. It's never just about pornography, or just about having affairs.

I think that sometimes we like to look at it and think that if we take the pornography away or if the Internet was not accessible then the problem is gone. But I think its more of a heart issue, and sometimes you can take the pornography away and you can take away that addiction and sometimes you will just move on to a new addiction. You have to look at it as a spiritual battle that is multidimensional.

Connie

Excerpt from the DVD <u>Freedom Begins Here: Personal Toolkit</u>. View this and other personal stories in their entirety in the special features portion of this DVD release. Available at many Christian Booksellers or online at www.freedombeginshere.org

DAY 11

IT'LL EAT YOU FOR LUNCH

"Get rid of all bitterness, rage, anger, harsh words, and slander, as well as all types of evil behavior. Instead, be kind to each other, tenderhearted, forgiving one another, just as God through Christ has forgiven you."

– Ephesians 4:31-32

Anger is an appropriate response to injustice, but when we don't resolve anger, it festers into bitterness, a negative state of mind that sours every relationship and distorts every goal. Many of us got into sexual sin to escape painful feelings in the past. In fact, a high percentage of sex addicts were sexually abused as children. Whatever the source of the pain, escape looks like an easy out. But escape doesn't let us deal with the reality of the pain stuck deep in our souls. While it is still stuck there, it continues to rot, to rob us of joy, to turn us into resentful, cynical people who delight in finding fault in others.

In his book *Wishful Thinking*, author and pastor Frederick Buechner described the bitter person's reason to live and the consequences of harboring resentment: "Of the Seven Deadly

Sins, anger is possibly the most fun. To lick your wounds, to smack your lips over grievances long past, to roll over your tongue the prospect of bitter confrontations still to come, to savor to the last toothsome morsel both the pain you are given and the pain you are giving back—in many ways it is a feast fit for a king. The chief drawback is that what you are wolfing down is yourself. The skeleton at the feast is you!"

Psychologists and physicians identify many different types of depression, but the most common can be termed "anger turned inward." That's another term for bitterness. Our bodies and souls can't cope with unresolved anger and bitterness for long periods of time. Sooner or later, they shut down and cease to function. Some people live for years with mild depression, but they still go to school or work each day. Others, however, become "clinically depressed" and are unable to function normally. They sleep too much or not enough, they eat too much or not enough, they are plagued by self-defeating thoughts and they feel utterly helpless and worthless.

Earlier in this letter, Paul told his readers to deal with their anger quickly so that it doesn't turn into bitterness and consume them. Here, he explains that we don't just forget the wrongs done to us; we forgive the offender. In forgiving, we often make one of two mistakes. We forgive too quickly when we allow ourselves to feel only the surface of the pain and jump to do the "right thing" to forgive and get the pain over immediately. The deeper wounds, though, stay ungrieved and unforgiven and the bitterness continues. Others, though, forgive too late. That is, they refuse to forgive at all because they can't imagine letting that person off the hook for the horrible thing he or she did.

We have a God-given, innate sense of justice and we can only forgive if we put those who have hurt us in the hands of God and trust him to deal with them. If we insist on retaining the right of vengeance, we harm ourselves more than we harm the offender. But if we put that person in God's hands and choose to forgive, we can be sure there will be a day when God asks the person for a full accounting—and that's enough for us.

Paul reminds us that we forgive others because Christ forgave us. The more we experience God's forgiveness, the more we'll be willing to forgive those who hurt us. And conversely, if we refuse to forgive, we need to experience Christ's forgiveness more deeply. Bitterness ruins lives. We need to be honest about the pain, focus on God's rich forgiveness for our sins and make the hard decision to forgive those who hurt us and put them in God's hands.

DAY**11** REFLECTION

Has your life been affected by bitterness? Explain.

_____

_____

What would it take for you to forgive those who hurt you? How would forgiving them affect your life?

_____

_____

DAY**11** PRAYER

Lord Jesus, you looked at all I've done and you've completely forgiven me. I want to climb out of the pit of bitterness. Today, I choose to forgive:

_____

_____

 # DAY**12**

ON YOUR SIDE

"'God opposes the proud but favors the humble. So humble yourselves under the mighty power of God, and at the right time he will lift you up in honor. Give all your worries and cares to God, for he cares about you."
– 1 Peter 5:5-7

Proud? That seems like a strange word to use in describing people who struggle with sexual sins, but it fits. No, they may not be proud of their secret behavior and their driving lusts for sex, but they demonstrate pride by trying to make life work on their own apart from the wisdom, love and power of God. That's the essence of pride: putting ourselves on the throne of our lives instead of putting God on the throne.

Those who engage in habitual sexual sin create their own world and they are the center of that world. They spend countless hours thinking about how to fulfill their most vivid desires and they use every moment of the day to fantasize, plan, act or hide all of these behaviors. They may have begun with a "harmless" hour looking at pornography or chatting with people who excited their sexual appetites, but before long, sex threatened to consume them. They feel alone, but strangely, they feel in control of their lives. God, if and when they think of him at all, is only a mosquito of a thought to be swatted away.

When we shove God out of our lives and pursue our own lusts—for sex, fame, possessions, power or anything else that takes his place in our lives—we find ourselves in a precarious position: God opposes us! When we read through Scripture, we see a stark picture of those whom God opposed. He went to great lengths to get their attention and if they refused to listen, he made sure he got their attention next time! God is slow to anger, but when it's time for him to move, he moves. We may feel like we're "getting away like a bandit" for a long time, but sooner or later, God will make himself known and it won't be a pretty sight.

Peter gave us both sides: God opposes those who insist on going their own way apart from God, but he allies himself with those who trust him. Do we want him on our side or against us? That's the question all of us have to answer. Peter had some difficult moments of pride in his own life, so he didn't want to leave us to figure out the answer on our own. He instructed us to humble ourselves before God and give him our worries. If we look to God for forgiveness, he will give it. If we go to him for direction, he'll guide us. If we trust him for strength, he'll put the power of his Spirit at work in us. That's his promise.

DAY**12** REFLECTION

What are some ways you've seen God oppose proud people who insist on going their own way apart from him?

_____

_____

Is God opposing you or giving you favor right now? Explain.

_____

_____

DAY**12** PRAYER

Oh God, everything in me wants to run from you sometimes, but I realize that you are the Creator and my Savior. You know best, and I sure don't. Right now, I bow before you and trust you to forgive me, lead me, and change me. I trust you to:

_____

_____

 # DAY**13**

COMING CLEAN

"'When I refused to confess my sin,

   my body wasted away,

   and I groaned all day long.

Day and night your hand of discipline was heavy on me.

   My strength evaporated like water in the summer heat.

Finally, I confessed all my sins to you

   and stopped trying to hide my guilt.

I said to myself, 'I will confess my rebellion to the Lord.'

   And you forgave me! All my guilt is gone."

   – Psalm 32:3-5

Human beings have an incredible capacity for self-deception. All of us, addicts and non-addicts alike, see what we want to see, hear what we want to hear and believe what we want to believe. For those who struggle with secret sins, self-deception becomes the normal way of life. Coming to grips with the depth of our sins challenges us to the core—but progressively opening our eyes to the reality of evil in our lives is an essential part of the healing, restorative process.

The recovery process has been compared to peeling an onion. Each revelation of our sin and the corresponding response of sorrow, grief, and forgiveness is followed by a time of relative quiet, but soon, God's Spirit taps us on the shoulder and points out yet another layer of rotten, stinking reality we've tried to hide for a long time. Quite often, we're shocked when we face the second layer. We think, "Man, I thought I was through with all that! What's this about?"

In his kindness, God doesn't show us the full weight of our sin all at once. If he did, we'd be devastated. To be honest, it's hard enough when he parcels out his revelations one at a time!

Don't be surprised that you have a second layer of pain and sin, and don't be surprised if God continues to reveal layers for a long time. How can you tell if you have more layers? In the powerful, personal psalm above, David says that he knew he hadn't "come clean" because of the physical and spiritual effects of the sin. He described eating problems, a nagging sense of fear and gloom and listlessness both day and night. These symptoms clearly told him that he needed to uncover and confess the sin he had buried and had tried so hard to forget.

As the layers are peeled off, we find that some of them are our blatant, selfish sins. We've turned our backs on God, hurt those we love, and cared only for ourselves. But other layers consist of the hurt we've experienced from others' sins and deep disappointments. Sins and wounds are both parts of the onion that need to be identified, peeled away, resolved and discarded.

Again in this psalm, we find a clear statement of God's faithfulness to forgive us if we agree with him about our sin. For each sinful layer represented by the onion, God's Spirit shines his light into the dark recesses of our lives where secrets have gone undetected. Exposure brings choices. At that moment, we can say, "No, the behavior or attitude really isn't that bad. And besides, everybody's doing it." Or we can respond, "Yes, Lord. You're right. That's selfishness and sin. Thank you for forgiving me."

The certainty of forgiveness is our motivation for confession, and confession brings relief from the debilitating spiritual and physical effects of continuing to harbor secrets. Coming clean happens in spasms of insight into the reality of our sins and wounds. Layer by layer, we experience more of God's love, forgiveness and strength.

DAY**13** REFLECTION

What are some physical and spiritual effects you've experienced from trying to keep your sins a secret?

_____

_____

How many layers have you seen and confessed? Is God pointing out the next layer now? If so, how are you going to respond?

_____

_____

DAY**13** PRAYER

Dear God, thank you for being so patient with me to point out sins and wounds layer by layer. I never realized how deeply sin and hurt have been residing in the crevasses of my life. Right now, I sense your Spirit pointing out:

_____

_____

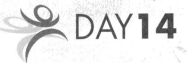

DAY**14**

IT'S ON ME

"Pay careful attention to your own work, for then you will get the satisfaction of a job well done and you won't need to compare yourself with anyone else. For we are each responsible for our own conduct."

— *Galatians 6:4-5*

One of the biggest hindrances of progress for those who struggle with sexual sin (or any habitual sin, for that matter) is an unwillingness to accept responsibility for their actions. It's much easier to blame somebody else—anybody else—for our sins and mistakes and many of us have perfected the art of shifting blame. We spend our lives trying to avoid anyone pointing out our faults, but on those rare occasions when someone confronts us, we loudly proclaim, "It's not my fault," "I couldn't help it" or "If you only knew what _____ (fill in the blank with the names of spouses, parents or whoever is available) did to me, you'd understand."

Yes, we've been hurt. People have sinned against us, sometimes wickedly and repeatedly, but often inadvertently because they were lost in their own selfish worlds just like we've been lost in ours. Those people are responsible for what they've done to us and we are, indeed, victims of their selfishness. But we don't have to remain victims. Today, we are adults and we have to take responsibility for our choices. One of our main choices is to stop the festering hurt inside us from dominating our relationships and decisions. That's up to us and it's our choice to make now.

Blaming others is an easy way out. It lets us remain passive, with all kinds of excuses for not moving forward, not resolving problems and not giving and receiving love. But blame-shifting ruins the relationships we treasure. Who can feel close to us when they fear that any problem we experience will become their fault?

In Paul's letter to the Galatians, he recognizes our tendency to compare our lives with the lives of others. He says, in effect, "Don't do it!" People who consider themselves to be perpetual victims resent people who haven't been hurt as badly and they resent those who have made progress to get over their hurts. Comparison feeds bitterness and the downward spiral of blame and depression spins out of control.

The solution is to "own" our feelings, attitudes and behaviors. We can stop blaming others for everything that happened to us in the past and everything that happens to us now. Instead, we can look at our lives through clear eyes and come to grips with our part in the drama. Others hurt us, but we have the responsibility to think rightly and act with courage and integrity. Instead of wallowing in self-pity and resentment, we can say, "I feel hurt and anger and I choose to forgive those who hurt me. I will talk to a friend to get some wisdom and I'll make better decisions in the future."

As we develop a track record of responsibility, we develop new habits of spending time with trustworthy people instead of those who lie and manipulate. Each new experience presents an opportunity for us to be responsible for our behavior and not blame anyone else. Soon, the habit of blaming others fades and the habit of accepting responsibility takes root. The backlog of resentment in our minds and hearts gradually goes down and in its place we develop a wealth of wisdom, joy and strength.

First, though, we have to recognize that blaming others is an excuse for avoiding responsibility for our painful feelings, resentment, and self-absorbtion.

DAY **14** REFLECTION

What are some examples in your life of comparison, blaming others, and avoiding responsibility for your feelings, attitudes and behaviors?

_____

_____

Describe what it means to take responsibility for these things.

_____

_____

DAY **14** PRAYER

Jesus, it's been easier for me to blame other people than to take responsibility, but I see the damage it's done to me, to my relationships and to my attitudes about everything in life. It has to stop. Right now, I want to take responsibility for

_____

_____

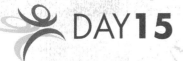# DAY 15

TRUST OR CONTROL

"Trust in the Lord with all your heart,

do not depend on your own understanding.

Seek his will in all you do,

And he will show you which path to take."

– Proverbs 3:5-6

We've spent our lives trying to make sense of things. We've obsessively controlled people and situations to prevent being hurt and to get what we want. Sometimes we've used the "carrots" of praise and gifts to win approval (and to keep people off our backs) and sometimes we've wielded big "sticks" of condemnation, cursing, slamming doors and other means of intimidating people into submission. We've lied to avoid the truth and we've exaggerated to impress. We've done all these things because we didn't feel safe enough to relax and we didn't trust that anyone would really care for us if they knew the awful truth.

If we can't trust, we have to control. There's no other option. Like a wounded animal, we are either on hyper-alert to notice even the hint of a threat from anyone or anything so we can react immediately and decisively, or we give up, become depressed and die inside. Obsessive awareness or passive hopelessness—one is evidence that we still think we can be in control if we try hard enough; the other is evidence that we have given up. Some of us flip-flop between these two extremes.

We may have ample reasons for not trusting this person or that person because those people have hurt us so badly and so often. Wisdom dictates that we keep our distance from them. But many of us refuse to trust even those who have proven they are trustworthy. It's like our "truster" is broken and it has to be restored before we can trust enough to feel safe, relax and overcome the compulsion to control.

To be honest, people are fallen and disappoint us from time to time. That's a given. However, God is perfect in wisdom, love, purity, and power. Trusting him doesn't imply that we're "in" on his reasons and ways of accomplishing his purposes. We may not understand all that he's doing, but we can always be certain that he knows, he cares, and he is working behind the scenes. Like a child who is confident of his father's love and strength, we recognize that we can't grasp all that God knows, but we rest in the fact that nothing surprises him and nothing is beyond his reach.

God is not just a little bigger and better than we are. He is infinitely great and good. He is the Creator, the one who spoke (he didn't sweat) and flung a hundred billion galaxies into space, each with 100 to 200 billion stars. He is also the one whose delicate touch created our bodies with minute precision. Medical science is now beginning to grasp its incredible complexity. God's goodness is demonstrated in his generosity, giving good gifts of life and possibilities to every person on the planet, even to those who despise him. The depth of his love, though, is most clearly shown on a hill two thousand years ago when his Son took upon himself all the sins of mankind to pay the price for our forgiveness.

God doesn't ask us to trust him blindly. No, he has given us countless examples of his trustworthiness by showing us his power and kindness. We don't have to depend on our ability to figure things out and we don't have to compulsively control people and situations any longer. We can look to God as his character is revealed in nature and in the Bible, and we can trust him.

DAY15 REFLECTION

What are some examples of the compulsion to control people and situations in your life?

_____

_____

What about God makes him trustworthy? What difference would it make if you genuinely trust him?

_____

_____

 DAY**15** PRAYER

Father, forgive me for trying to control everything and everyone around me instead of trusting you. You are trustworthy, and I praise you for:

_____

_____

MARK'S STORY

> ## "We heal through the sharing of stories when we find out that we are not alone."

The first thing I normally do is just tell my own story. We heal through the sharing of stories when we find out that we are not alone.

I believe in surrounding people with other hopeful examples of the fact that you can do this. I think one of the great theological or spiritual challenges is to confront your pride.

Mark

Excerpt from the DVD Freedom Begins Here: Personal Toolkit. View this and other personal stories in their entirety in the special features portion of this DVD release. Available at many Christian Booksellers or online at www.freedombeginshere.org

# DAY**16**

TRIGGERS

"The temptations in your life are no different from what others experience. And God is faithful. He will not allow the temptation to be more than you can stand. When you are tempted, he will show you a way out so you can endure."

— Corinthians 10:13

"How could I be so stupid?"

"I thought I could stop. What happened?"

"I never saw it coming. One minute I was doing fine, but then I gave in again."

These statements of despair are echoed thousands of times a day by men and women who gave in again to temptation. They had good intentions and many of them had a track record of staying sexually clean and sober before they fell again. What happened? We are creatures of habit, but habits aren't just behaviors. They have a neurochemical element as well. Like Pavlov's dog, when something "rings our bell," we jump to act because we've been rewarded and because the sound of the bell emits chemicals in our brains that stimulate our desires. Habits, especially those involving sex and drugs, are hard to break. We have to recognize the "triggers" that tempt and stimulate us and we need to avoid them at all costs.

Triggers in the lives of people who struggle with habitual sexual sins may be particular people whom have seduced us or we have seduced, places we've been that brought sexual thrills, or things that remind us of sexual exploits. Particular words or descriptions of body parts can send us flying in the wrong direction. Songs on the radio remind us of times when we felt particularly excited. Particular movies and television programs can set us off, too. Almost anything associated with sexual thrills—especially secret sexual thrills—can trigger desires and tempt us to act out again.

The promise in Paul's letter to the Christians in Corinth is that God won't allow us to be tempted beyond our capacity to say "no." The urges are incredibly powerful, but God has given us even more powerful resources. We simply need to recognize them and use them. The first resource is avoidance. We need to get away from people, places and things that trigger us. Before you say, "That's impossible," consider the consequences of giving in again and rethink your answer. We have choices and one of our choices is to stay away.

All day, every day, we have countless discretionary decisions about what we see, what we hear and what our minds dwell on. Change channels, put in an uplifting CD or DVD, throw away those magazines and books (yes, those too!) and feed your mind things that are good and right and noble. Good choices about these things are our second resource in overcoming temptation.

We won't make it far in our recovery from sexual sin if we try to do it alone. The third resource is a friend, sponsor or counselor we can call any time of the day or night to ask for help. One man called his sponsor every day after work on his way home because he drove past a strip joint and he wanted his sponsor to hold him accountable not to pull off the highway and go in. It worked.

God's provision to help us avoid falling into temptation isn't magic. We don't pray a secret prayer or wave a magic wand. We can avoid exposure to most of our triggers if we make better choices, and temptation won't get the better of us if we have a strong, wise friend who will help us through the rough spots.

DAY **16** REFLECTION

What are some specific triggers for you?

_____

_____

What are some ways you can avoid each one? Name some
better discretionary choices you can make. Who is a friend who
will hold you accountable?

_____

_____

DAY **16** PRAYER

Dear God, I need to be more shrewd about protecting myself
from temptation, and I need to have somebody to keep me
accountable when times are tough. Today, I'm making these
lifestyle changes to minimize triggers in my life:

_____

_____

 # DAY **17**

DON'T EVEN THINK ABOUT IT

"Instead, clothe yourself with the presence of the Lord Jesus Christ. And don't let yourself think about ways to indulge your evil desires."

— Romans 13:14

If you spent an hour with the president or a king, you'd make sure you were on your best behavior, wouldn't you? Or if the governor or mayor asked you to come for lunch, you'd be honored and you'd be careful to say and do the right thing. Those scenarios can seem very farfetched and unlikely, but the truth is far more alarming: We are in the presence of Jesus Christ, the King and Creator of the universe, all day, every day—and he's not distracted in the least!

God isn't a benevolent grandfather who looks the other way when the kids misbehave, and he isn't Santa Claus, who has only wonderful gifts for everybody. Scripture depicts God as both infinitely kind and awesomely powerful. Over and over again, we read that he is both Judge and Savior. As Judge, God isn't dispassionate like judges in our court system. He passionately

FREEDOMBEGINS**HERE**

defends right and avenges wrong. He serves as the prosecutor who asks penetrating questions, and if someone is found guilty, he is the executioner. All roles are found in him as the Judge. As our Savior, however, Jesus Christ has taken the full, horrible weight of our sins upon himself. We deserved eternal death because of our selfish sins, but he is our substitute, paying the price for us. This is the one, both righteous Judge and courageous Savior, in whose presence we live all day, every day.

Paul tells the Romans to "clothe" themselves in Christ's presence. We may do many things to win the approval of some people or to avoid being honest with others, but we can never escape the all-seeing eyes of Christ. He knows all of our actions, our heart's attitudes, and our deepest thoughts. When we forget that we live in the presence of "an audience of one," we think we're getting away with our sexual sins (and all the other kinds of sins), but that's ridiculous. His presence surrounds us like a blanket, or in Paul's phrase, like a robe enveloping us. We forget that fact at our own peril.

The reality that we live in Christ's presence motivates us to do right and terrifies us from doing wrong. That's Paul's point. If we would watch our words and actions in the presence of an earthly leader, how careful should we be in the presence of the Creator, Savior, Judge and King?

Evil desires? Yes, we've had them, and to be honest, they still lurk in the corners of our minds. In this passage, Paul doesn't say,

"Don't give in to temptation," and he doesn't warn us, "Watch your attitude." Instead, he draws the line all the way back at the beginning of our thoughts: "Don't let yourself even think about it!"

Some of us have great reverence for God, and we're motivated to please him because he has done so much for us. We realize that Paul's instructions begin with our thoughts because our thoughts are fertile soil for our actions—for good or for evil. Other people, though, don't feel a lot of gratitude toward God. Their emotions are far different. They are terrified of his impending judgment! Fear, however, is a powerful motivator, and if we are indulging in willful sin, fear of God's righteous judgment is entirely appropriate.

Recognize that Christ is fully present with you every minute of the day. Think, choose, and live accordingly. If Christ is your Savior, thank him for his loving, wise guidance. If you haven't trusted in Christ to forgive you, he stands as judge to exact vengeance, but he extends his hand of forgiveness as Savior. Take it.

DAY **17** REFLECTION

How do you feel when you think about being in Christ's presence all day every day?

_____

_____

What changes do you need to make so that you live under his gaze and make him smile?

_____

_____

DAY **17** PRAYER

Jesus, it stuns me to realize you have been present when I've done the things I've done—yet you still love me and forgive me. That's amazing. I want my life to make you smile. To do that, these are the things that I need to change:

_____

_____

DAY **18**

TRUE FRIENDS

"Brothers and sisters, we urge you to warn those who are lazy. Encourage those who are timid. Take care of those who are weak. Be patient with everyone."

– 1 Thessalonians 5:14

We've laughed about them in the past. We've ridiculed them for being so narrow and rigid. We've avoided eye contact with them and we've kept conversations superficial. They are people who have conquered their sexual sins and those who have developed strong, healthy relationships. If the truth is known, we've hated them because they made us feel so uncomfortable. But now, as we struggle to make changes in our lives, we're learning to value their wisdom. It's a big change for us.

How can you tell if someone is a true friend? When we were involved in habitual sins, we thought our friends were the people who went to strip clubs with us, laughed at our jokes, accepted our lame excuses for bad decisions—and worse, celebrated our bad choices! They made keeping secrets a lot easier because they had so many of their own secrets and they trusted us to keep theirs, too. Secrets, lies, self-deception, denial, ridiculing others and covering tracks—those were the elements of those "friendships."

When we talk to a counselor, a friend in recovery or a sponsor, we see the contrast. Our new friends don't celebrate our sexual conquests. They grieve for us. New friends have a strong, powerful blend of truth and grace. They talk about the reality of their struggles and the wonder of God's grace to love and accept them every step on their journey toward wholeness. Sometimes, they say hard things to each other and, we're finding out, they say hard things to us. When we make excuses for our sins and blame others, they shake their heads and say, "No, you have to own it yourself." We hate to hear those words, but we begin to listen because we see how far they've come. They've earned our respect. When we don't understand, they don't criticize us for being stupid. They've been down the same road before and they know how hard it is to take the steps we're taking. When we need a hand, they are glad to extend theirs to steady us.

In the early months of change, the world seems to be turned upside-down. Long-buried emotions bubble to the surface (or explode) and we don't know what to do with them. Our new friends assure us that we aren't going insane—it's all part of the healing process. As we change, our family members feel very uncomfortable and wish we'd go back to the way we used to be; or as we confess our sins, they may lash out at us in rage for hurting them so deeply. At those moments, emotional health and good relationships seem like they are a million miles away, and we want to give up. Our new friends, though, come alongside to encourage us, support us and give us some of the wisdom they've learned. From them, we learn to hang on and grow stronger.

The transition from old friends to new ones is crucial and threatening. If we don't make new connections, we feel so isolated, so alone, so vulnerable. Frankly, many people quit at this point. At this pivotal moment, we need to muster the courage to go to someone and say those words we've avoided for so long: "I need your help."

It will make all the difference in the world.

DAY **18** REFLECTION

Describe the attraction of staying with old friends and the risk of finding new ones in recovery.

____

____

Now describe the attraction of new ones and the risk of staying with the old ones.

____

____

Do you have a new friend you can trust? If not, where can you find one?

_____

_____

DAY **18** PRAYER

Lord, I really need somebody to help me. Thank you for those people who are farther down the road and can help me. Today, I will reach out to:

_____

_____

 # DAY**19**

REWARDS

"But the wisdom from above is first of all pure. It is also peace loving, gentle at all times, and willing to yield to others. It is full of mercy and good deeds. It shows no favoritism and is always sincere. And those who are peacemakers will sow seeds of peace and reap a harvest of righteousness."

– James 3:17-18

All of us are motivated by rewards, but they don't all have the same impact on us. Some rewards reinforce poor behavior and some motivate us to build healthy habits. Let's not mince words. Sexual sin has plenty of rewards: the thrill of the chase, the rush of planning our exploits in minute detail, the release of orgasms and the challenge of keeping secrets. This description makes it sound like a James Bond movie, which is another part of the allure.

If sexual sin didn't give us thrills, we'd find something else, but these pursuits come at a steep price. We live under a constant cloud of suspicion, or at least the threat of being caught. Our obsession with sex absorbs our time and attention, so we neglect our work, our spouse and our kids. We spend money on ever-increasing thrills and mounting debt can stare us in the face. We live a double life and the strain to keep the lies straight can overwhelm us. Because of the strain, many of us indulge in added addictions to alcohol, illegal drugs, prescription drugs, gambling or anything else that numbs the pain or heightens the thrill. Each thrill reinforces our habit, but we need more and more to satisfy us.

If you look in the faces of men and women who have come out of the darkness of sexual sin and into the light of God's forgiveness and restoration, they talk about a completely different set of rewards:

"I don't have to explain what I did last night anymore. I can look my wife in the eyes without flinching."

"I never dreamed my husband would forgive me, but he did. Our relationship is better now than it ever was before I slept around."

"My children respect me now. They know what I did, but they also know that I've worked hard—really hard—to change. They appreciate that."

"I was depressed. I was thinking about suicide because I didn't know if there was any way out of the mess I had created. But God rescued me, and today, I have more peace and purpose than I could have imagined."

"When I first came clean about my sexual sins, I had a long, long way to go. Now I'm helping other people who are where I was. It's a privilege."

"I have to be honest. I always used people to get what I wanted and I didn't care how much it hurt them. I was the most selfish person in the history of the world, but God didn't leave me like that. He changed me. Today, I have real relationships—the kind where people laugh because we're relaxed and cry because we care. It's amazing."

James wrote that wisdom has great rewards in our own hearts and in our relationships with others. People in recovery are on the road to wisdom. Every step of the way, they learn hard lessons about the pain of making dumb choices and the beauty of giving and receiving authentic love. Instead of manipulating people, they build relationships based on trust. Trust, though, must be earned and they're earning trust with every good decision they make.

Someday, all of us who stay on the path of healing and hope can look back and thank God for the changes in our lives. It's always a rocky road, but it's a journey each of us can travel with a little courage and a lot of help. Before long, we realize that others are

looking to us for help, and we have the honor of extending a hand
and helping them take the next step.

🏃 DAY**19** REFLECTION

Describe the rewards of sexual sin and the rewards of a changed
life.

_____

_____

Which of the rewards of change motivate you most strongly?
Explain.

_____

_____

🏃 DAY**19** PRAYER

Dear God, I've been such a fool. I thought it was so much fun
to destroy my life and hurt the ones I love. Forgive me, Father.
Thank you for those who are examples to me of wisdom, joy,
strength and hope. The reward I'm most motivated to achieve
is:

_____

_____

# DAY**20**

OVERWHELMED WITH GRATITUDE

"When a certain immoral woman from that city heard he was eating there, she brought a beautiful alabaster jar filled with expensive perfume. Then she knelt behind him at his feet, weeping. Her tears fell on his feet, and she wiped them off with her hair. Then she kept kissing his feet and putting perfume on them. . . . [Jesus said to the host of the dinner,] 'I tell you, her sins—and they are many— have been forgiven, so she has shown me much love. But a person who is forgiven little shows only little love.'"

– Luke 7:37-38, 47

"I deserve better." That's a sentiment that inevitably leads to resentment. We utter that phrase when we believe we've gotten the short end of the stick, and then our hearts become hardened and we live with a chip on our shoulders. We expect (actually, we demand!) that everybody we know treat us with the utmost respect and appreciation and we insist that they overlook all of our faults.

A more accurate and healthy perspective is the realization that as fallen human beings, and as those whose sexual sins have wounded others, we deserve eternal condemnation. Justice dictates that we go "where the worm does not die and the fire is not quenched." That's what we really deserve! But thankfully, that's not the end of the story.

We've received God's fabulous mercy and grace. These are two very important concepts in our transformation. Mercy means that we don't receive what we deserve: We escape God's righteous wrath. Grace involves mercy, but it goes a step further: We receive a status as God's beloved children on whom he delights to shower his goodness and reveal his greatness. When we have even the slightest grasp of the height and depth and length and width of God's mercy and grace for sinners like us, we are amazed at his love.

Scripture uses many pairs of people to illustrate distinctly different responses of demands and gratitude. Jesus told a story about two men praying in the temple. One was overwhelmed with his need for forgiveness; the other believed he deserved God's blessings because he had been such a good person. The brokenhearted, repentant man, Jesus explained, is the one who received and enjoyed God's forgiveness.

Luke tells us about when Jesus was invited to dinner at a religious leader's house. At some point earlier in the day or the week, Jesus had encountered an "immoral woman," and she responded to his gift of forgiveness. When Jesus and his men were in the leader's house at a formal dinner, the woman, quite uninvited, was so overwhelmed with gratitude that she came to anoint Jesus feet with perfume and wash them with her tears. This woman's response, Jesus explained to the demanding, hardhearted host, is entirely appropriate for someone who has experienced God's cleansing love. The woman knew her sins had earned only condemnation, and she was thrilled that Jesus had forgiven her! Nothing could stop her from expressing her authentic, overflowing appreciation to him.

Our words are measuring sticks of our attitudes. Do we say, "I can't believe he did that to me. I deserve better!"? Or do we say, "I can't believe God could forgive me for the things I've done. I deserved hell, but he has given me forgiveness, love, and hope!"?

DAY**20** REFLECTION

What are some ways our demands ruin our attitudes and rob us of thankfulness?

_____

_____

Does the immoral woman's response to Jesus reflect your appreciation for his mercy and grace toward you? Explain.

_____

_____

# DAY**20** PRAYER

Lord Jesus, forgive me for being so demanding and not
realizing what I really deserve because of my sins. I want to
sense the depth of your mercy and grace like this woman did.
Thank you so much for:

_____

_____

LAMAR'S STORY

"They accepted me and encouraged me and I moved forward a step."

What really changed my life were the moments when I could be honest with people. They accepted me and encouraged me and I moved forward a step. And these were baby steps. That's all that anybody can take — just baby steps. We're not going to rebuild our reputation, our relationship with our wife, our peers, our bosses, whoever, in one grand step.

The moments that helped me the most were the ones when I was the most vulnerable and the most loved.

Lamar

Excerpt from the DVD Freedom Begins Here: Personal Toolkit. View this and other personal stories in their entirety in the special features portion of this DVD release. Available at many Christian Booksellers or online at www.freedombeginshere.org

# DAY**21**

"WHO DO YOU SAY THAT I AM?"

"When Jesus came to the region of Caesarea Philippi, he asked his disciples, 'Who do people say that the Son of Man is?'

'Well,' they replied, 'some say John the Baptist, some say Elijah, and others say Jeremiah or one of the other prophets.'

Then he asked them, 'But who do you say I am?'

Simon Peter answered, 'You are the Messiah, the Son of the living God.'"

– Matthew 16:13-16

Ultimately, this is a question each and every one of us must answer. One day, we will stand before Christ and he will ask the same question he asked those who followed him two thousand years ago: "Who do you say that I am?"

Jesus, though, didn't wait until he had come out of the tomb or until the disciples died to ask them this question. He asked it in the middle of his time with them as they interacted with him and saw him touch the lives of others every day. Jesus doesn't wait to ask us, either. Today and every day, he asks, "Who do you say that I am?"

Our words may say "the Christ, the Messiah, my Savior," but our lives reflect our authentic answer. Obedience—or the lack of it—proclaims our heartfelt beliefs. Do we see Jesus as just a kind man or a wise teacher, or maybe someone who was powerful two thousand years ago but absent today, or just a guy with some great ideas, or maybe our grandmother's God, but not ours? If we put him on the level of Buddha or Thomas Jefferson, we can take or leave his commands to us because they don't carry any real weight.

If, though, we really believe that Jesus Christ is the Creator, the one who is "far above all," and the most awesome being in the universe (and beyond), then we'll sit up and pay attention to his directives. Jesus walked this earth for a while, bound by time and space, but he is no longer bound in this way. In one of the most graphic descriptions of Christ found in the Bible, John, perhaps Jesus' best friend on earth, had a vision of the risen Savior. In the first chapter of Revelation, John gropes for words to tell what he saw: Christ's head and hair were white like snow, his eyes "like blazing fire," his feet glowed like molten metal, and his voice sounded like a crashing waterfall. John was so overcome with the awesome sight that he fainted! Today, Jesus isn't walking the earth, and he isn't limited by flesh, time or space. He is far more like John's description of him in Revelation, so overwhelming that to grasp a glimpse of his majesty would cause us to faint.

Do we yawn when we think of Jesus, or do we marvel at his greatness and grace? When we were absorbed in our sinful acting-out, we tried not to think about him at all, but now God is in the process of changing our lives and our view of him makes all the difference in the world. When we face difficult choices, we need to remember that the ever-present Christ is with us to help us. When we feel hopeless, we can think about Christ's power and creativity to weave even the black strands of our lives into a beautiful tapestry of hope. When we are oppressed by shame, we remember that when the risen Jesus appeared to Thomas, he showed Thomas the holes in his hands and the wound in his side that were inflicted when he died on the cross to forgive even the most horrible of our sins.

Who do we say Jesus is? It's not a flippant question, and the answer will determine our response to him every moment of every day.

DAY**21** REFLECTION

How would you have answered that question when you were in the midst of your sexual sins? How would you answer it today?

_____

_____

What's the link between our view of Christ and our obedience?

_____

_____

DAY**21** PRAYER

Christ, you are awesome. You are far greater and far more gracious than I can ever imagine. You deserve my loyalty, my love, and my obedience. Today, I will honor and obey you by:

_____

_____

 DAY**22**

THE REAL THING

"Don't just pretend to love others. Really love them. Hate what is wrong. Hold tightly to what is good. Love each other with genuine affection, and take delight in honoring each other."

– Romans 12:9-10

For too long, we used people instead of loving them. We used anger to control them and we withdrew from them to punish them and to protect ourselves. Our secret lives consumed us, and gradually, we became completely absorbed in our own little worlds. After a while, we didn't even know what was going on in other people's lives; to be honest, we didn't care. The only thing that mattered was whether they kept their mouths shut instead of confronting us about our sins.

Manipulation and self-protection, however, are poor substitutes for love. Beneath our fear of being exposed, we long for the real thing. We want to cast off the pretenses and deceptions. We want what every human being longs for: to love and to be loved.

The transition from control to love doesn't happen in an instant. Two kinds of changes are necessary—changes in us and changes in those around us. We have to come to grips with the fact that we've messed up our lives and left a huge vacuum by our self-absorption and we've pushed away the most cherished people in our lives. Now our selfishness is repulsive to us and we're determined to change. We begin by reaching out, speaking words of kindness, and offering acts of service. Quite often, though, our first attempts at reconciliation are met with a cold stare—or rage!

The other change that must occur is in our family members, friends and co-workers who have every reason in the world to believe that our new, positive, loving behavior is a fraud. To convince them, our commitment to change needs to be tenacious, persistent and patient.

The first attempts in expressing genuine love and appreciation almost certainly will seem awkward. Don't let that stop you! Think about what it will mean to earn people's respect so they drop their guard and let you back into their lives. Consider what can happen in your marriage and in your relationship with your children. Let your mind drift back to the happiest times you spent together when you talked and laughed and enjoyed being together. Times like those can happen again, but now they'll be different—even richer than before. The path to restored love is through the door of forgiveness. You will ask for it, and they will give it—maybe not at first, and maybe not until you've demonstrated that you are serious this time about changing. And when forgiveness is expressed and accepted, incredible things can happen. Instead of secrets, fear, anger, hurt and self-protection, we "delight in honoring each other." Instead of looking out only for our own interests and lusts, we look for ways to affirm, to encourage, and to praise.

Sooner or later, people see through pretended love. Because love promises so much, they feel doubly disgusted at the fake. Pornography and sexual acts aren't love at all—they're not even close. But now it's time for a new beginning, a time to learn or relearn what it means to care more for others than we do for ourselves. People—you and the people around you—are hungry for the real thing. Don't settle for anything less.

DAY22 REFLECTION

How would you describe "pretend love"? How is it different from the real thing?

_____

_____

What is one thing you can do today to show real love to someone?

_____

_____

 DAY**22** PRAYER

Oh God, my love has been phony. I've cared far too much about me instead of loving those around me. Please forgive me. Your love is strong and constant. I need to soak it up. I need to let it change me at the core of my soul. Lord, today, I choose to show real love to _____ by:

_____

_____

 DAY**23**

REBUILDING TRUST

"Meanwhile, Zacchaeus stood before the Lord and said, 'I will give half my wealth to the poor, Lord, and if I have cheated people on their taxes, I will give them back four times as much!'

Jesus responded, 'Salvation has come to this home today, for this man has shown himself to be a true son of Abraham.'"

– Luke 19:8-9

Words. People have heard us proclaim long and loudly that we were going to change and that things were going to be different, but nothing changed. Oh, we may have made a few halfhearted attempts from time to time, and people believed us. We thought we could get away forever with not really changing, but now we realize we've damaged our reputation and robbed our relationships of trust—the glue that holds them together. People are tired of our words, and if we're honest, we know they're right. We're tired of all the lies, too.

Luke tells us about a man who was despised by his neighbors. Zacchaeus was a tax collector who extorted money by making people pay more taxes than they owed. He put the difference in his own pocket. He met Jesus, and the people complained that Jesus didn't have any business hanging out with scum like the little, conniving tax collector. But Jesus delighted in changing lives—especially the lives of those considered to be beyond hope—people like Zacchaeus, and people like us. Meeting Jesus, though, wasn't bland, flavorless religion for Zacchaeus. Jesus touched the deepest recesses of his heart and transformed a selfish man into a thankful, generous one.

Zacchaeus put his money where his mouth was. He repaid those from whom he had extorted money, and he gave half of his money to the poor—the ones who had bitterly complained about Jesus having dinner with him! (Imagine the expressions on their faces!) Zacchaeus wanted to rebuild trust with people he had hurt and offended, but it took more than words.

In our lives, too, words alone won't count for much. People have heard them before and they've become jaded at the sound. Trust must be earned and so far we haven't earned it. Even the first few steps aren't enough to win the confidence of people who have heard our lies time and time again. What will it take to rebuild trust? It depends on how badly trust has been eroded or shattered by our sin, but it will take enough truth being told, enough right actions being repeated and enough time to prove that the changes are real.

Does that seem unfair? Does it feel like people should trust and respect you because you have new, good intentions and you've taken a step or two of change? Trust is the most precious and sacred part of any relationship. We don't throw it around easily or take it lightly. When we trust someone, we relax because we feel safe and we are confident because that person has proven that he or she is competent and consistent. The first steps of recovery only begin the process of rebuilding trust. If others have difficulty trusting you, don't blame them. It's not their fault. Sure, they may resist trusting you and they may be slow to have confidence that the changes are real, but they have every reason to be suspicious. Give them a break and give yourself a shot of reality. It's going to take time.

Rebuilding trust doesn't need to be a guessing game. Perhaps you already know what you need to do to prove yourself to others, but perhaps not. If you aren't clear, you can ask, "What can I do to build trust between us?" After you ask, be quiet and listen. You may get quite an earfull! Don't be defensive. Instead, treasure the person's honesty and willingness to engage in this conversation. Listening is a huge steppingstone to understanding, and understanding is vital if trust is going to grow.

DAY**23** REFLECTION

What are realistic expectations for you and for those you've hurt as you try to rebuild trust?

_____

_____

What are three things you can do this week to take steps to rebuild trust with people in your family, with your friends and with anyone else you value?

_____

_____

DAY**23** PRAYER

Jesus, I want to be like Zacchaeus. I want my actions to match my words so that those who complain most bitterly (with good reason) about me will know that my commitment to you is real. Help me, God. I need your wisdom and strength as I take these steps. This week, I want to take these steps:

_____

_____

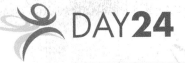 # DAY**24**

NO WASTED PAIN

"We can rejoice, too, when we run into problems and trials, for we know that they help us develop endurance. And endurance develops strength of character, and character strengthens our confident hope of salvation. And this hope will not lead to disappointment. For we know how dearly God loves us, because he has given us the Holy Spirit to fill our hearts with his love."

– Romans 5:3-5

One of the most wonderful (in the true sense of the word) promises in Scripture is that God is willing to use every difficulty in our lives, no matter the source, to enable us to grow wiser, stronger and humbler. For many of us, this concept is very difficult to grasp because, when we're really honest, we have to admit that the vast majority of the pain in our lives is self-inflicted. Yes, others have hurt us, but we've made some colossal blunders that have severely wounded those we love and we have ruined our own lives. Can God redeem even that? Yes, he can, and yes, he will, if we'll trust him to do it.

When we don't grasp God's intention to use pain for good, we avoid it at all costs. God, however, doesn't let us off that easily. We may deny it, minimize it, rationalize it or justify it as long as we can, but sooner or later, our pain catches up to us. Then it's time to pay attention. Author C. S. Lewis said that pain is "God's megaphone" to get our attention. We may run from God as long as we can, but when the pain of our sins and hurts is too big to handle, we look up for help.

J. I. Packer, professor and author of the classic book *Knowing God*, observed that God has a higher purpose than helping us avoid pain. Packer wrote, *"This is what all the work of grace aims at—an even deeper knowledge of God, and an ever closer fellowship with Him. Grace is God drawing us sinners closer and closer to Him. How does God in grace prosecute this purpose? Not by shielding us from assault by the world, the flesh, and the devil, nor by protecting us from burdensome and frustrating circumstances, nor yet by shielding us from troubles created by our own temperament and psychology; but rather by exposing us to all these things, so as to overwhelm us with a sense of our own inadequacy, and to drive us to cling to Him more closely. This is the ultimate reason, from our standpoint, why God fills our lives with troubles and perplexities of one sort or another—it is to ensure that we shall learn to hold Him fast."*

When Paul wrote to the believers in Rome, he wanted to communicate a message of hope about the suffering they encountered. Nothing could give them more confidence in God than to realize that he uses every painful event to produce endurance, strength of character, and confident hope. These things follow in this order: First, we have to buckle down and cling to God because we don't know what's going on. In the midst of our desperate trust in God, his Spirit works wonders in our hearts so that we value truth, courage, love and kindness. As we experience character transformation, we grasp more deeply that God has been at work all along—even when we didn't realize he was there—and confident hope swells in our hearts. None of this, though, happens because we figured it out on our own. God has been at work behind the scenes, from getting our attention to the transformation of our hearts—and we are deeply thankful for it.

At the beginning, God's purposes in our pain aren't the same as ours. We want to run away, but he wants to use our pain to change us. We are wise to catch on quickly.

DAY**24** REFLECTION

What are some ways God has gotten your attention through the megaphone of pain?

_____

_____

What difference does it make in your attitude and outlook to realize that God wants to use everything in your life—even your past sins—to transform you?

_____

_____

DAY24 PRAYER

Dear Father, it seems almost unimaginable that you would use my darkest moments for good, but that's what this passage promises. Today, I need to endure by _____ _____ and you want to chisel my character to produce _____ _____ so that I have a strong hope in you.

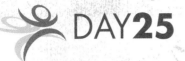

DAY**25**

THE THRONE OF GRACE

"So then, since we have a great High Priest who has entered heaven, Jesus the Son of God, let us hold firmly to what we believe. This High Priest of ours understands our weaknesses, for he faced all of the same testings we do, yet he did not sin. So let us come boldly to the throne of our gracious God. There we will receive his mercy, and we will find grace to help us when we need it most."

– Hebrews 4:14-16

To fix our lives, we're tempted to look for a magic formula, a secret bullet or a global answer that will solve all of our problems instantly, but that's not the way life works. Spiritual life is a long walk, not a ride in the space shuttle! On that hike, we take one step at a time and our steps are tens of thousands of little choices to pursue God, to choose right instead of wrong, to pray, to speak the truth, to talk to a friend, to extend kindness, and to help people.

For centuries, Christians have used time-honored practices in their quest for God. Those who have grown strong in their faith have developed patterns of life to regularly study the Bible, pray, enjoy close friendships with believers and serve those who are less fortunate. Too often, we've seen those habits as dead and dry sources of guilt, but that is a gross misunderstanding of those things. God invites us to his side, to his throne, to spend time with him to soak up his truth and grace. Bible study and prayer are ways we connect with God and they are two of the most profound privileges he has given his children. The writer to the Hebrews reminds us that Jesus experienced all the same hurts and temptations we feel, but he didn't sin. Still, he understands us better than we understand ourselves and he invites us to hang out with him so he can convince us that he loves us more than we can imagine.

Reading the Bible isn't some odd, mysterious activity. It is God's Word to us, and if we read it with an open heart, his Spirit uses it to expose sin, convince us of his forgiveness, remind us of his purposes, keep us on track and encourage us every step of the way. But if we're not reading and reflecting upon it, we drift along wondering why the Christian life doesn't work for us.

Prayer and Bible study go together hand-in-glove. As we pray, we can reflect on passages of Scripture we've just read and pray them back to God. For example, we can use Paul's prayer in the beginning of his letter to the Colossians that God would fill them with the knowledge of his will with all spiritual wisdom and understanding so that they would walk in a way that pleases God. As we pray, we think about what it means for God to show us his will for specific situations and relationships, for him to guide us, and for us to make decisions that make him smile. That's a meaningful prayer!

Some people complain that the Bible was written thousands of years ago to a very different culture. That's true, but its insights about our hearts and our relationships are as relevant as today's online news. If we want to be close to God, we need to pray. If we want to grow in wisdom, we need to reflect on God's truth. To grow strong in our faith, we need to develop good daily habits that include both prayer and Bible study. Don't have time? We make time for things we think are important. What could be more important than growing in wisdom, character, and closeness to God?

DAY 25 REFLECTION

What has been your motivation for working through this devotional?

_____

_____

What can you do to make prayer and Bible study a habit? What might that look like? What would work for you and your schedule?

_____

_____

 # DAY**25** PRAYER

Dear God, you have invited me to come to your throne and
spend time with you, and you've given me your word to unveil
your heart and your purpose for my life. I treasure those things,
but God, I want to treasure them far more. This is what I want
to do to make prayer and Bible study a habit:

_____

_____

DAY**26**

LIVING IN TENSION

"For you have been called to live in freedom, my brothers and sisters. But don't use your freedom to satisfy your sinful nature. Instead, use your freedom to serve one another in love."

– Galatians 5:13

Who can forget the closing scene of the movie *Braveheart* when William Wallace was being tortured and executed for leading a rebellion against the evil English king? Even at the moment of his greatest pain, he still longed for his countrymen to experience something he was giving his life for: Freedom!

All of us long to be free. Those of us who struggle with sexual sins want to be free—completely free—from lust, from shame and from the devastating impact of our sins. In other words, we want to be free from struggle. That, however, isn't what the Bible promises when it says we've been called to live in freedom. God has freed us from the bondage of sin. Paul loudly proclaimed, "There is now no condemnation for those who are in Christ!" For those who committed small sins? Yes. For those who lied to those they love? Yes. For those whose sins are too unspeakable to mention in public? Yes, for them, too. In another letter (Colossians 2:13-15), Paul said that our forgiveness is similar to being freed from prison. The punishment we deserve was written on paper that was nailed to our cell door, but Jesus took the paper with our list of sins and nailed it to his prison, the cross, where he paid in full the price for all of our sins. We weren't excused. God didn't say, "Oh, your sins weren't that bad." They were so bad that they deserved death, and that's precisely the price Jesus paid for them. Our cell door is open and we are free!

The question is: What do we do with our freedom? While we're in this life, we have a foot planted in two worlds. We have been set free and we are called children of God, but we still struggle with our old nature of lust and evil desires. Now, though, we have a new motivation. In the past, we were self-absorbed, wanting to satisfy our darkest desires at any cost, no matter who we hurt. But now we've been set free from the guilt and shame. Every moment of every day, we now have a choice, to please God or to pursue our lusts. Paul instructs us in the passage above, "Don't use your freedom to satisfy your sinful nature. Instead, use your freedom to serve one another in love."

We won't be completely free from sinful desires until we see Jesus face to face and the transformation begun here is completed. In the meantime, God has given us weapons for the fight and a goal to achieve. We have forgiveness and freedom from guilt, the truth of God's Word, and the Spirit's presence and guidance every step of the way—if we'll listen. We no longer wander through life seeking selfish pleasures. Now we have a new goal, a new purpose and a new passion: to please the one who took what we deserved, who suffered in our place and who died to pay the price for our sins.

Like any new skill, it takes time for us to learn to live in freedom and to develop new habits that please God. We have hundreds of choices each day to feed and nourish our "black dog" of selfishness and sin or our "white dog" of God's forgiveness, hope, love and service.

Which dog are you feeding?

DAY**26** REFLECTION

What are some ways to help us realize that we live in tension in this life instead of expecting complete freedom from lustful desires and the consequences of sin?

_____

_____

Which dog are you feeding? Explain.

_____

_____

 # DAY**26** PRAYER

Dear Jesus, thank you so much for paying the price to open my prison door to set me free. I want to experience that freedom and I want to use my freedom to please you. Today, I'm going to feed my "white dog" by:

_____

_____

LANCE'S STORY

"Do I still have the itch for it? Absolutely."

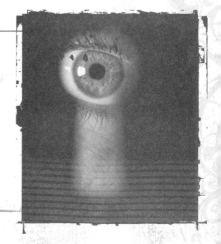

Do I still have the itch for it? Absolutely. As my anxiety goes up throughout the daytime I have an itch for pornography. I know that the accountability software is on my computer. I can't go to it. I can trust these people that are my accountability partners. I can call them on the phone and say "Hey, I'm hurting. I'm itching. I'm really wanting to look at porn." And they've prayed with me and they walk me through it.

Lance

Excerpt from the DVD Freedom Begins Here: Personal Toolkit. View this and other personal stories in their entirety in the special features portion of this DVD release. Available at many Christian Booksellers or online at www.freedombeginshere.org

 # DAY**27**

THE PROCESS OF GROWTH

[Jesus said,] "Those who accept my commandments and obey them are the ones who love me. And because they love me, my Father will love them. And I will love them and reveal myself to each of them."

– John 14:21

Some people sit in churches for years and wonder why their spiritual lives remain so dull and drab. Others go to seminars, Bible studies and even recovery groups, but their lives don't seem to change. It's discouraging and confusing. What's missing?

To be painfully honest, some of us have strained out any parts of God's Word that required change in our lives. We were simply too invested in our selfish lifestyle to listen. But now we're ready and we want the real thing, nothing phony or halfhearted. We've come to a place where we are desperate for God to work in our lives to redeem the past, to give stability to the present and to provide hope for the future. We're ready for change! The key to growth, Jesus tells us, is our willingness to take action to obey him.

The Christian life (and especially recovery from addictions and compulsive behaviors) was never meant to be a spectator sport. Throughout Scripture, we see God giving invitations and commands and people choosing to obey—or not. Jesus looked at Peter and Andrew and said, "Follow me." They dropped their fishing nets and followed him. The Holy Spirit directed Paul to go from one city to another. Whether it seemed reasonable or not, and whether it was convenient or not each of these people obeyed. The New Testament contains hundreds of clear commands for believers to follow. They deal with choices in our values, our lifestyles, and our relationships. They address virtually every element of life. Jesus explained that there is a direct link between our response to these commands and our growth in experiencing his presence more deeply.

In our world today, obedience has gotten a bad reputation. The word conjures up images of force and feelings of guilt, but we need to understand that obedience is a reasonable response to wise direction from someone who loves us more than we can imagine. As we grow in our wonder at the infinite wisdom, love and power of God, we'll trust him more and we'll gladly obey him more. It's that simple. Is God worthy of our loyalty (which is another word for obedience in action)? Each of us has to answer that question, but Gospel writers show us that Jesus was incredibly kind, attentive, gracious, wise and powerful. Though his followers were sometimes confused, the 11 who obeyed "got it" and devoted every fiber of their lives to him. That's appropriate loyalty and glad obedience.

What is Jesus telling us to do? He has given us commands to speak truth, to love authentically, to turn from evil, to forgive those who hurt us, to show kindness to others, to run from opportunities to sin, to spend time with people who passionately want to follow him, to regularly study his word, to develop a pattern of prayer, and to fight every day to stay on track in our recovery. We can find a million excuses why we don't obey, but in the final analysis, not one of them counts. Obedience, especially in the early stages when change is so radical, requires courage. Take heart. He's with us every step of the way.

Jesus promised that if we'll obey him, he will open the doors of heaven so that we experience the presence of God more richly than we ever dreamed possible. We listen, we obey, and our relationship with him deepens so that we hear his voice whisper to us through Scripture and by his Spirit more clearly and more often. Like his early followers, we'll sometimes still be confused, but the pattern of our lives will be marked by listening and following, not by self-protection and selfish actions.

 ## DAY**27** REFLECTION

What are two or three specific commands God has given you?

_____

_____

What can you expect (sooner or later) from God and from yourself as you take action to obey God?

_____

_____

 ## DAY**27** PRAYER

Lord Jesus, I've been too slow to obey. Forgive me. Help me grasp your greatness and goodness more fully so that I obey more gladly. Today, I will take steps to obey you by:

_____

_____

DAY**28**

THE PLEASURE OF A CLEAR CONSCIENCE

"Run from sexual sin! No other sin so clearly affects the body as this one does. For sexual immorality is a sin against your own body. Don't you realize that your body is the temple of the Holy Spirit, who lives in you and was given to you by God? You do not belong to yourself, for God bought you with a high price. So you must honor God with your body."

– 1 Corinthians 6:18-20

A man in recovery reported, "One of the biggest changes in my life has been the freedom from oppressive, morbid, shameful, self-destructive thoughts. Before I met Christ and started growing in my faith, my mind was consumed with all that stuff. I relived past events and conversations all day, every day, trying to justify what I'd done or condemning myself for them. It was my own mental hell. Now, though, I rarely go down that road at all."

For people who struggle with sexual sin, the mental gymnastics of denial and rationalization can be amazing! We go to great lengths to convince ourselves that what we're doing is reasonable and normal, but occasionally (for some of us) or quite often (for others), the reality of the shame overwhelms us, and we hate ourselves for being so messed up.

The recovery process shakes up our previous thought patterns, exposing them to the light of truth and love. We quickly realize that we've devoted countless hours to fruitless mental pursuits, hours that weren't just wasted, but that caused genuine harm. Our pursuit of sexual sin poisoned our thoughts, devastated our families, and for some, affected their bodies with sexually transmitted diseases and debilitating depression.

Now, though, we have choices. We can continue to let our minds sink into the pits of sexual images or shame, or we can latch our thoughts on to God's truth, his love and his wonderful purposes for us. As we develop new habits of thinking, we learn to attack the oppressive thoughts with good, godly, positive concepts. Instead of spending hours complaining in our heads about how rotten life is, we focus on the gifts of forgiveness, sunlight, people who still care for us and the chance to live another day with fresh hopes. Gradually, we put new "books" of healthy thoughts on the bookshelves of our minds, ones that we can pull out any time we need them—like when we are tempted to lie, engage in sexual sin or grovel in shame. These encouraging volumes come from many sources: Scriptures, wise sayings of trusted friends, insights from books and our own journaling when God gave us new understanding.

A clear conscience is a beautiful thing—in fact, it's an amazing thing for those of us whose minds had been packed full of garbage but who now experience lightness and life. We now know God loves us, forgives us and accepts us, not because we've been perfect, but because he has poured out his grace upon us. When we sin now, we don't deny it and bury it. When the Spirit taps us on the shoulder and says, "Hey, that was sin," we agree, "Yes, you're right. Thank you for forgiving me."

We are overwhelmed with the incredible fact that we were hopeless and helpless, but now we have been bought with a steep price. We aren't our own anymore, and we're glad about that.

DAY28 REFLECTION

How would you describe your thought life up to this point?

_____

_____

What are some elements and processes God uses to give us a clear conscience?

_____

_____

 # DAY**28** PRAYER

Oh God, my thoughts have been a disaster! I've lied to myself
and to you, and I've wallowed in self-pity and refused to accept
your forgiveness. But it's different now. I'm learning to be
honest about my sins and to embrace your forgiveness and love.
Lord, I want to fight against the lies I've believed. Today, I want
to identify some new "books" to put on the bookshelf of my
mind:

———————————————————————————

———————————————————————————

DAY**29**

JOY ON THE ROAD

""Purify me from my sins, and I will be clean;

wash me, and I will be whiter than snow.

Oh, give me back my joy again;

you have broken me—

now let me rejoice."

– Psalm 51:7-8

When we face the brutal reality of our sins, our fragile pride is shattered. We've lived a secret life for months or years, using anger, lies and manipulation to keep people from the truth and to control them. When anyone got too close, we insisted, "I'm fine," "Nothing's wrong," and "I didn't do that! Don't you believe me?" But now, we have faced the truth and our pride is broken to bits like a delicate vase dropped on a tile floor.

When we are broken, we have a choice: to stay shattered, hopeless, and helpless, passively giving up and blaming others for our problems, or trusting God for forgiveness and restoration. One is cowardly; the other is courageous.

King David committed two awful sins: adultery and murder. He tried to hide, but Nathan confronted him with the truth. David's response to God is captured in this beautiful, powerful psalm. In it, he doesn't excuse himself or blame anybody else. He is painfully honest about his sins, and he expresses his trust that God will forgive and restore him.

When we were neck-deep in our sexual sins, we pursued pleasure at all costs. We experienced sexual and emotional release and we felt strong when we conquered someone sexually—either in our minds or in reality. The chase was as much fun as the deeds and our elaborate efforts to hide from others accentuated our pleasures. Secret sins, we concluded, are even more delicious.

All of these pleasures, however, are counterfeits for true joy. They stimulate and titillate, but the price we pay for them includes ruined reputations, shattered trust, isolation, degradation, shame and self-hatred. The joy God gives when we repent is 180 degrees in the opposite direction. We walk in light because we don't have to hide anymore, we give and receive love instead of using people, we bask in God's forgiveness instead of denying our sins or wallowing in shame and we realize our lives can count for something meaningful instead of being wasted on meaningless pleasure. That's real joy!

Joy, though, isn't found just at the end of the trail when we've gotten every element of our lives ironed out. We can experience joy every step of the way from the first moment we express our sorrow to God and trust his promise to forgive us. At each step, in every moment of every day, we face choices to keep going with God or to veer off into selfishness again. Old habits die hard, so don't expect perfection. Each time we grab an old habit by the throat and strangle it by saying "No!" we take a step toward God and toward restoration—and each of these steps is a reason to celebrate!

Yes, the process of recovery involves some gut-wrenching choices, but the journey also includes many wonder-filled moments when we realize more deeply than ever how much God loves us—even us! We find a few true friends who understand us, who know the worst about us and who stand by us anyway. And gradually, God restores relationships we feared had been lost forever. God smiles on us at every step, and as we feel his pleasure, we experience a deeper joy than ever before.

DAY**29** REFLECTION

Describe your experience of being broken. What motivated you to trust God to forgive and restore you?

_____

_____

FREEDOMBEGINS**HERE**

What are some things you can do (by yourself or with others on the journey) to experience more joy along the way?

_____

_____

☓ DAY**29** PRAYER

Father, facing the truth shattered me, but you are putting the pieces back together again. I can't thank you enough! I want to experience true joy each step of the way. To refresh my sense of joy in your forgiveness and purpose, today, I'm going to think about:

_____

_____

 # DAY**30**

NEXT STEPS

"I don't mean to say that I have already achieved these things or that I have already reached perfection. But I press on to possess that perfection for which Christ Jesus first possessed me. No, dear brothers and sisters, I have not achieved it, but I focus on this one thing: Forgetting the past and looking forward to what lies ahead, I press on to reach the end of the race and receive the heavenly prize for which God, through Christ Jesus, is calling us."

– Philippians 3:12-14

Progress, not perfection. Steady growth, not instant change. Patience and persistence, not unrealistic expectations of complete, instantaneous healing. These phrases describe Paul's perspective about his own spiritual journey and certainly they apply to our recovery from habits of sexual sin.

Many of us feel tempted to live in the past, to go over our shameful acts again and again to punish ourselves for being so stupid and selfish, but Paul encourages us to focus on a hopeful future. We've trusted God for forgiveness, and we've started out on a new path. Now, we "press on" by making choices each moment of each day to trust God even more. As we walk with him, amazing things happen to us. We've experienced a taste of joy, freedom and health, but there's a lot more to come. Just imagine what it will be like to develop strong habits of dwelling on truth so that we have a settled mind. Just imagine what it will be like to experience God's grace even more deeply so that we feel—in the depths of our souls—God's love, forgiveness and acceptance. Just imagine what it will be like to enjoy relationships based on trust, respect and honest communication. And just imagine what it will be like when we don't have to look over our shoulders all the time because we're afraid of being caught.

The recovery process is like rehab for a broken arm. At first, we have to realize the damage that's been done and seek help. The doctor puts our arm in a cast to stabilize it, and for weeks, our lives are consumed by the reality of our pain. Gradually, the pain subsides, the cast is removed and the long rehab process begins. Day after day, the weakened muscles are stretched and strengthened. Some days, we want to quit because it hurts so bad, but we realize that we'll always be crippled if we quit, so we muster the courage to keep going one more day. Each day, we become stronger, more mobile and our actions become more natural. In the same way, we need to have realistic expectations for our growth and change in recovery from sexual sins. Healing won't come instantly, but we'll see real progress if we stay with our own version of rehab.

In your spiritual, emotional and relational rehab, what are the next steps? If you haven't found a friend, sponsor, support group or counselor, be sure to do that soon. People don't make good progress without someone's help. You might want to read one of Dr. Mark Laaser's books, *Healing the Wounds of Sexual Addiction* or *Faithful and True*. Find resources (music, sermons, conference messages, online articles, etc.) to fill your mind with things that are "true, honorable, good, right and lovely." Our attitudes and actions are products of what's going on in our minds, so latch your thoughts on to God's truth and stories of hope and courage. The principles we've addressed in this book challenge us and inspire us, and they never get old. You'd probably benefit from going through this devotional again soon, and maybe again a few months from now. You might realize that God is doing some amazing things in your life!

God has given you courage to take bold steps. No matter what happens, don't stop. He has some wonderful things in store for you!

DAY**30** REFLECTION

Describe the similarities between rehab for a broken arm and the process of recovery from sexual sins.

_____

_____

Describe what you "just imagine" God might do in your heart and relationships in the coming months.

_____

_____

What are the next steps for you? When will you do them?

_____

_____

DAY**30** PRAYER

Oh Father, you are so gracious to me! I'm just beginning the process of healing and restoration, and I trust you'll keep encouraging and guiding me. My next steps are:

_____

_____

BILL'S STORY

"The thing that kept coming to my mind was that I deserved death and I received mercy."

The thing that kept coming to my mind was that I deserved death and I received mercy. And this wasn't about the marriage. This was about me being right with God.

I cannot imagine living my life a different way today. Because of the transparency now, I didn't have any secrets so for the first time in my life I didn't have to hide.

Bill

Excerpt from the DVD *Freedom Begins Here: Personal Toolkit*. View this and other personal stories in their entirety in the special features portion of this DVD release. Available at many Christian Booksellers or online at www.freedombeginshere.org

GOING **DEEPER**

So you've finished your 30-day journey and you want to know more. We have assembled some teachings from the "Freedom Begins Here: Counselor ToolKit" to help you learn even more about finding freedom from sexual sin.

3 **SPIRITUAL** QUESTIONS

"Here a great number of disabled people used to lie— the blind, the lame, the paralyzed. One who was there had been an invalid for thirty-eight years. When Jesus saw him lying there and learned that he had been in this condition for a long time, he asked him, 'Do you want to get well?'"

– John 5:3-6

First Question:
"Do you want to get well?"

Your first instinct may be to feel labeled or diagnosed by your family and friends. We see in the above passage that Jesus had a different initial response. It was a question that cut to the heart – simple, yet powerful. This is a question each of us must face. Be honest with yourself – do you really want to be free?

Second Question:
"What are you thirsty for?"

"Jesus answered, 'Everyone who drinks this water will be thirsty again, but whoever drinks the water I give him will never thirst. Indeed, the water I give him will become in him a spring of living water welling up to eternal life.' The woman said to him, 'Sir, give me this water so that I won't get thirsty and have to keep coming here to draw water.'" (John 4:13-15)

You have heard of a God-shaped vacuum that exists within each of us. It cannot be denied. Since the beginning of time, people have sought to fill it. King Solomon had indescribable riches, multiple lovers, extensive accomplishments, unparalleled wisdom and people who waited on him hand and foot. He built a vast kingdom, grew intricate gardens, taught multitudes of people and conducted intensive studies. Yet in all of this, he felt empty.

He wrote "I denied myself nothing... yet when I surveyed all that my hands had done and what I had toiled to achieve, everything was meaningless" (Ecclesiastes 2:10 & 11). His conclusion in the end was this: "Fear God and keep his commandments, for this is the whole duty of man" (Ecclesiastes 12:13). Solomon realized one could never fill the void inside with things the world has to offer. We were made to love God and to be loved by Him in Christ.

Jesus used the analogy of thirst because he knew that every need of man – whether physical or emotional – points to the deepest need of man, which is Christ. God designed us in such a way that our physical and emotional needs are all manifestations of some aspect of our spiritual need for Him. We thirst for water, but our real thirst is for a spring of living water unto eternal life. We desire pleasure because moments of bliss give us a taste of heaven. We long for sex, which points to our deep desire for intimacy, connection and pleasure – all characteristics of our eternal home.

If you can look past the behaviors to see the real need, you can fill it with Christ. Follow up the question "What are you truly thirsty for?" with "What is the true source of quenching that thirst?" Christ quenches all thirst.

Third Question:
"What are you willing to die for?"

"Jesus called in a loud voice, 'Lazarus, come out!' The dead man came out, his hands and feet wrapped with strips of linen, and a cloth around his face. Jesus said to them, 'Take off the grave clothes and let him go'" (John 11: 43-44).

When Jesus heard Lazarus was sick, "he stayed where he was two more days" (verse 6). Once he knew Lazarus was dead (verse14), Jesus and his disciples went to where Lazarus was. The family and friends of Lazarus were weeping in devastation from the loss. Jesus became "deeply moved in spirit" and wept as well (verses 33, 35).

This story evokes a few questions: Why did Jesus wait until Lazarus was dead? If he already knew Lazarus was dead and already knew he would rise again (verse 23), what was he lamenting?

Jesus knew Lazarus' death was for the purpose of God's glory (verse 4). He knew it was allowed for the benefit of the people – so they would believe (verse 15). But there was also a principle birthed out of the story. Lazarus could not be resurrected unless he first *died*. He could not be released from the grave clothes unless he first was put in the grave. So, too, we must fully die to ourselves before we can be resurrected by the power of Christ.

He cannot raise us to new life if we are still living for ourselves. When Jesus saw the people's sadness, he was overcome with compassion. Though Lazarus would be resurrected, it did not take away the pain experienced in the moment by all who loved him. The sight of weeping moved Jesus, but he probably was lamenting something beyond just that scene—the sadness and loss of the human experience.

You will need to come to a place of total surrender—of dying to self, old patterns, old solutions and old behaviors. Christ will not leave you in the grave. Though he may tarry, he will come once you have reached the place of death. His arrival may take time (Lazarus experienced the grave for four days), requiring patience and faith. But Jesus comes with healing and compassion in his hands. He does not expect you to clean up before he comes (he did not care about the smell of Lazarus' grave; see verse 39). He wants to deliver because of his great love! Resurrection, total healing, complete freedom and recovery can and will happen with Christ. Ask yourself, "What are you willing to die for?"

"The power of the resurrection can only be made manifest when we are willing to die to ourselves."

– Mark Laaser

THE **PROCESS** OF CHANGE

"Change in the Christian life is progressive."

– Dr. Larry Crabb

If you want to be well, if you know what you're thirsty for, if you are willing to die to yourself in order to get it—then you are ready for the journey of change. Change most often takes time. It is a process. Christians are daily being conformed to the image of Christ—it does not happen all at once. It is true that the moment we believe, we are instantaneously transformed into the kingdom of light (Colossians 1:13), raised with Christ and seated with him in the heavenly realms (Ephesians 2:6) and given the seal of the Holy Spirit (Ephesians 1:13). Still, we have to be renewed day by day. We are constantly striving toward the goal of becoming who we were meant to be. The apostle John phrased it this way: "Dear friends, *now* we are children of God, and what we *will be* has not yet been made known. But we know that when he appears, we shall be like him, for we shall see him as he is. Everyone who has this hope in him *purifies himself*, just as *he is pure*." (1 John 3:2-3) Our standing in Christ is that we are already pure because we will be made like him—but in light of this hope, we engage in the process of purification. Think of a sunflower. The seed of a sunflower is still a sunflower, though it is a seed. It does not change in the sense of *what it is*, it only changes in the sense of *what it looks like*. We can greatly benefit from focusing on who we are meant to be—indeed, who we are—while going through the process of change to become that person. A blueprint of that process was laid out for us in the book of Exodus. Below is a diagram by Virginia Satir of steps toward change:

The Process of Change
by Virginia Satir

Stage 6: New Status Quo

Stage 5: Practice

Stage 4: New Integration

Stage 3: Chaos

Stage 2: New Information (or Foreign Element)

Stage 1: Status Quo

Satir, V. Banmen, J., Gerber, J., & Gomori, M.,
The Satir Model: Family Therapy and Beyond,
1991, Science & Behavior Books, Inc. Palo Alto, CA

Stage One:
Status Quo (Egypt)

Sexual sin has been a method of coping with a famished soul for years. It is how you've gotten by. You begin the process of change in a state of oppression.

The Israelites were also in bondage. Their status quo was slavery to the Egyptians. They got to that place because of a famine and remained slaves for decades.

Stage Two:
New Information (Moses & The Red Sea)

If you're struggling, it often takes outside intervention to help you realize your degree of addiction. King David did not fully recognize the depth of his sin until the prophet Nathan confronted him (2 Samuel 12). Nathan described one who had done wicked things; then he said, "You are the man!" Sometimes it takes someone else coming to us and spelling out the things we have done in order for us to see clearly. If your sin is plainly defined as what it is, then there is a better chance you will respond as David did: "I have sinned against the Lord." (verse 13)

The person who intervened for the Israelites was Moses. He went to the Israelites and told them what the Lord had commanded him to do concerning their deliverance (Exodus 4:30). It was new information, it was risky, it required faith and courage—at first they responded, saying, "Leave us alone; let us serve the Egyptians." (Exodus 14:12) They were scared. They were unbelieving. They were not thirsty enough. But God changed their hearts—they decided to take a step of faith. Their enemy Pharaoh resisted. They were hotly pursued until they could go no farther—they reached the edge of the land, which met the Red Sea. The enemy was approaching. What could they do? Nothing. But God did something. He met them there and parted the sea so they could complete their exodus.

We might be scared at first; we may not want to give up our sin. When we reach the place of surrender we will, like the Israelites, meet obstacles. The enemy will come after us once we decide to change. Satan will not want to let go—indeed, all the years of struggle have been years under his control. Be encouraged and look to God when you hit a wall and feel the enemy approaching. The Lord will provide a way through the obstacle, as Moses said to the people, "The Lord will fight for you." (verse 14).

Stage Three:
Chaos (The Desert)

Once all of our old coping patterns are out of the picture, our lives may feel quite chaotic. Coming out of sexual strongholds requires major adjustment—it can shock the system. Sometimes it feels like the new environment is worse than the old.

The Israelites at times longed to go back to Egypt. The desert wasn't so great. It was hot, it was hard and they didn't know what they were going to eat day after day. There was much complaining and self-pity (16:2). God heard their grumbling and gave them the command to gather enough manna for the day's need. It was the principle of depending upon the Lord one day at a time.

We also must take it one day at a time. The feeling of chaos will pass, but perseverance is required to get through it. We need faith to get out of the desert. When the Lord wanted to bring the Israelites into the Promised Land, Moses sent ten spies into Canaan to take a look. Only two came back ready to possess what God was going to give them—the other eight came back fearful and ready to return to Egypt. There were great giants in the land and the Israelites did not want to deal with the next obstacle; because of their unbelief, those men died in the desert.

God wants us, like Caleb and Joshua, to continue to hold on to his promises. We must believe that we have the victory and not show contempt to the Lord because of the obstacles we face. Follow after Caleb, who said to his fellow men, "We should go up and take possession of the land, for we can certainly do it." (Numbers 13:30) God looked upon him and was pleased, and because of Caleb's faith, he inherited the promise, "Because my servant Caleb has a different spirit and follows me wholeheartedly, I will bring him into the land he went to, and his descendants will inherit it." (14:24)

Stage Four:
New Integration (The River Jordan)

As we push through the obstacles, we will enter another level where new strategies and techniques will need to be integrated. This level requires a higher degree of vulnerability, accountability and risk-taking. Group sessions, couple counseling, daily contact with a sponsor, working out the twelve steps, Bible studies and whatever other necessary steps are all crucial to reach healing.

The Israelites needed to cross the Jordan River—it stood between them and the Promised Land. This was a new level of vulnerability. The Jordan had a strong current, flowing downstream into the sea. When they came to it, it was at flood level because it was harvest time (Joshua 3:15). Crossing would be life-threatening.

But the Lord told them to cross in order to reach Canaan. The Israelites had to trust and obey—it was the only way to succeed. As the priests set foot in the waters, the river piled up ahead of them and stopped flowing where they were. The entire nation crossed on dry land.

The river did not dry up until they took the first step—it was a step of faith. All they knew was that they were stepping into very strong waters that could easily overcome them. A new schedule will sometimes look like a strong current that could rush over our heads. We need not walk by sight but by faith. As we do, we will see the Lord stepping in and giving us what we need. The Lord will give us that extra strength to go to yet another meeting—not before we leave but after we are on our way. The Lord will give us the words to be vulnerable with our accountability partner, not before we pick up the phone but as we open our mouth. The Lord will work to take away the fear and anxiety.

Stage Five:
Practice (Ongoing Battle)

With all the information we receive from Bible studies, books, counseling sessions and talks with our accountability partners, we will have a lot of new things to put into practice. We will learn how to set new boundaries and set new standards. We will learn how to identify false beliefs in a moment of temptation.

We will learn how to have healthy relationships—with God, our spouse, others and ourselves. We will be encouraged toward new physical and spiritual disciplines. We will learn to surrender daily to Christ and fill ourselves with the Word. All of these things will need to be practiced. They should be carried out until the new behaviors become more familiar than the old.

The Israelites crossed the Jordan with very clear instructions from the Lord. Since the Numbers account tells of the spies sent to scout out the Promised Land, the following book of Deuteronomy is nearly wholly devoted to specific instructions from the Lord concerning what they were to do after crossing the Jordan. That is a lot of new information! Their next move was to carry it out. The battle of Jericho was a huge success because the Israelites put into practice what the Lord had taught them to do. Now that they had the land, it was extremely important they adopt the behaviors God showed them. The new strange land needed to become home.

The new place of obedience and surrender needs to become home for us. It needs to be practiced constantly until it becomes second nature—more natural than the old place of bondage and addiction.

Stage Six:
New Status Quo (The Promised Land)

Once we have consistently practiced different behaviors, new habits will form and change will take place. As we integrate all aspects of the healthy sexuality model and its various suggestions of behavior, a transformation occurs. Truth overwhelms our former false perceptions. Darkness is swallowed up by light. Neurochemical pathways in the brain are restored to healthy levels as our mind is renewed and pleasure centers and thought patterns are literally transformed (Romams 12:2). As we continue to steadfastly resist the devil, he will flee in recognition of his defeat (James 4:7-10). We will, like the Israelites, reach a new status quo. The Israelites reached Canaan and were no longer slaves to Egypt. They were no longer wanderers in the desert; they were no longer without a home. The goal is that we come to the place where we are no longer in bondage to sexual sin, and are no longer wandering through the ups and downs of healing. Once we are set free, it does not mean we can lay down our armor and kick up our feet. The Israelites had years of fighting in order to gain possession of what God had already given them—and to this day they remain on guard defending it. It will forever be the same with us. God has given us freedom in Christ, but we will have to claim it and take it from the enemies who do not want to let us go. After taking possession, we should defend it daily, never dropping our guard or becoming lazy. As Paul urged the Ephesians, we too should be encouraged:

"Be strong in the Lord and in his mighty power. Put on the full armor of God so that you can take your stand against the devil's schemes. For our struggle is not against flesh and blood, but against the rulers, against the authorities, against the powers of this dark world and against the spiritual forces of evil in the heavenly realms. Therefore put on the full armor of God, so that when the day of evil comes, you may be able to stand your ground, and after you have done everything, to stand." (6:10-13)

It will involve a daily surrender to Christ. It will involve realizing that it is God who works in us to be all we are meant to be. Consider the following verses:

"Now to him who is able to do more than all we ask or imagine, according to *his power that is at work within us*." (Ephesians 3:20)

"Being confident of this, that he who began a good work in you *will carry it on to completion* until the day of Christ Jesus." (Philippians 1:6)

"It is God who *works in you to will and to act* according to his good purpose." (Philippians 2:13)

"And we pray this in order that you may live a life worthy of the Lord and may please him in every way: bearing fruit in every good work, growing in the knowledge of

God, *being strengthened with all power according to his glorious might* so that you may have great endurance and patience." (Colossians 1:10-11)

"Guard the good deposit that was entrusted to you—guard it with the *help of the Holy Spirit* who lives in you." (2 Timothy 1:14)

"We know that anyone born of God does not continue to sin; the One who was born of God *keeps him safe*, and the evil one cannot harm him." (1 John 5:18)

 **CREATING** A VISION

"One of the central parts of the spiritual dimension, of making a change and of trusting God more is the ability to create and hold onto a vision for your life."

– Mark Laaser

The writer of Proverbs declared, "Where there is no vision, the people perish" (29:18, KJV). Helen Keller, when asked what would be worse than being born blind, replied, "To have sight without vision." This section has been adapted from the Professional Counselor Edition of *Freedom Begins Here* in which Eli Machen discusses the importance of realizing God's calling and creating a vision consistent with our purpose. Machen emphasizes the need for a vision that goes beyond sobriety, stating, "Recovery is about something greater than trying to stay sober."

Rick Warren wrote in The Purpose Driven Life, "Living on purpose is the only way to really live. Everything else is just existing." He encourages readers to develop a purpose statement for their life in order to cultivate and maintain vision.

You can be encouraged in the same way, starting with some simple questions. Take time to write out your answers:

According to Scripture, what are God's purposes for your life?

What would you like to do with your life?

What do you not want to do?

What things, people or ideas in life are most important to you?

What is success?

What are the desires of your heart?

What are your greatest strengths?

What motivates you?

What is the center of your life?

Who are you going to live for?

What kind of person do you want to be?

What do you want your life to contribute?

What do you want your life to communicate?

At the end of it all, when you stand before Christ, what things in your life are going to matter?

Your answers may overlap—this indicates key elements in the development of your vision. A vision, according to Machen, is a clear mental picture of a preferable future—what's more, this future is not only preferable, but also possible. Why form a purpose statement or create a vision? What makes it so important? It is a matter of motivation.

Motivation: Need vs. Vision

We are motivated by two things:

1. Need
2. Vision

When we are motivated by need, we often will do no more than we have to. We will do only what it takes to get by. Take, for instance, the person who has been "found out" by his spouse, boss or church family. He is presented with an ultimatum: Give this up or _____. Fill in the blank—it could be "we are going to get a divorce" or "you are going to lose your job." These may prove to be powerful motivators at first, but in time the enemy can creep in and present thoughts like, "Is my marriage or job really worth all of this work?" Eventually, all of the meetings, counseling sessions, daily phone calls and spiritual disciplines become monotonous. Seeking recovery out of the following reasons—

(1)   appeasement (to please others)

(2)   dependency (because of our need for others)

(3)   control (as a means to control others)

(4)   manipulation (to influence outcomes)

—makes us more vulnerable to failure. Change is best motivated by something deeper: a heart that sincerely desires it.

With a genuine heart, a lot is possible. When thinking about what generates heartfelt sincerity, we are brought back to vision. Vision compels us, giving hope, strength and energy.

Think of walking through a completely dark tunnel. You do not know where it ends. Your steps are slow. You cannot see where you are going. You become more easily discouraged. Now think of that same tunnel with a light at the other end. The end is in sight. The path before you is lit. You walk briskly, with confidence that you are going to make it out.

People who do not believe they will make it have no vision of the end. They are clouded by the darkness—negative self-talk, self-esteem and core beliefs—continually being triggered back into early trauma. Perhaps because of these things they have never seen success. Negative emotions keep them trapped in unhealthy behaviors.

Go back to the first experience when you started to believe the lies. Once in that place of trauma, try to visualize Jesus there.

Ask, "What is he saying to me now?" Replace the lies with biblical truth of who you are, how God views you, and the purposes for your life. Remind yourself of these things daily. You have a choice—you can choose to believe the lie or the truth. You do not have to be as you have always been. There is another option. It starts with God's Word—reading it daily renews our minds with truth in the midst of earthly reality. Think of Peter stepping out of the boat to meet Jesus on the water. The earthly reality was that he could not walk on water and that there were stormy waves all around. God's truth was that Jesus was there, and because of that, Peter could do anything.

There is light at the end of the tunnel—being in God's Word helps us visualize it. The light chases away darkness, providing hope and motivation.

THREE FRUITS OF VISION

When you have vision, it is demonstrated in three things:

1. Determination
2. Commitment
3. Passion

Vision breeds a determination. It says, "I'm willing to do whatever it takes." You know the journey is about something greater than individual, droning steps. Each one leads to a bigger purpose.

Vision breeds commitment. It is a heart decision that does not stray. When Daniel was taken captive to Babylon, he resolved not to defile himself with the king's choice foods. This commitment was made before the time of temptation. The King James Version puts it this way: "Daniel purposed in his heart not to sin." (Daniel 1:8) It was a covenant Daniel made with himself and God in the secret chamber of his heart. A genuine desire to change helps us envision the goal and set our hearts on finishing.

Vision breeds passion. Seeing that the end is attainable will spark an incredible output of energy and inspiration. When we redirect our vigor for sexual pursuits into healthy avenues, we will be amazed at our potential.

Once you have formed a purpose statement/vision (based on previous questions), ask, "Are your life choices congruent with your vision?" It is vital for us to realize that our choices have gotten us to the place we are. In the same way, new choices can get us to an entirely different place. We often assume the way we are is just the way it is. There is no other option. This is baloney! Anyone who wants to can completely change course.

Every success story, every achievement, every triumph has started first in the mind. Michelangelo, concerning one of his most famous sculptures, stated, "I saw the angel in the marble and I carved him until I set him free." Ask yourself, "What do I see in the marble? What in me needs to be set free?"

After generating a desire for vision in the heart, cultivate that vision in the mind.

Eli Machen says, "Your type of life determines character, character determines appetite, appetite determines vision." In other words, who are you? What is in your heart? What are you hungry for? Are you looking for those things that will satisfy that hunger? A buzzard is a vulture (type of life)—by nature this bird feeds on carrion (character). Because of this he has a desire for dead, rotting flesh (appetite). This kind of appetite causes him to be on the lookout for roadkill and other kinds of dead animals (vision). What have you been looking for? That determines what you have been hungering for, which determines your character because of the life you have lived. Unlike the buzzard, you can control and change all of these things by surrendering to God.

THREE STEPS IN HEALING

1. My vision is inadequate and my life is out of control.
2. I must turn control over to God.
3. I must turn my life over to God's vision of who I am.

The Israelites did not believe they could take the Promised Land because they saw themselves as grasshoppers. They did not submit to the vision that God had for them. He saw them as his chosen people, dependent on him and—because of that—successful. But they forgot his mighty working power and focused instead on false self-beliefs. That kept them from possessing what they were made to have. It was their children who took the risk of seeing themselves in a different way. They had the vision of going into Canaan as warriors who would take over the land—and that is exactly what they did.

We need to let go of the self-view we have always had and take hold of God's view. How does he see us? Why do we exist? Who are we supposed to be? Visualize that man or woman. We do not have to be confined to the old patterns. We have two options: (1)—Stay in the desert and see yourself as a grasshopper (earthly reality), or (2)—Go into the Promised Land and refuse to believe that you "can't" (God's Truth). Once a surrender of perspective takes place, God will use his vision and power to carry us through to the promise.

☘ THE **HEALTHY** RECOVERY **CYCLE**

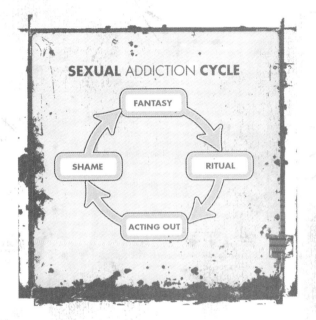

Leading sex therapist Dr. Patrick Carnes first described the sexual addiction cycle in his book *Out of the Shadows*. The cycle starts with powerful, negative core beliefs we have about ourselves— usually evoking feelings of shame. In order to cope, we develop a fantasy life to escape painful feelings and create desired outcomes. Fantasy and preoccupation lead to rituals. A ritual is anything we do from the first thought of sexual activity to the actual acting out. The ritual itself can be addictive. For example, you may go to a bar in order to seek out a sexual experience. In the meantime you have several drinks to lessen apprehension.

This ritual, if done enough, can lead to alcoholism.

Rituals can also involve much simpler activities—like staying up until everyone else has gone to bed in order to look at Internet pornography. Rituals can be short or long, depending on the sexual activity. They can last a matter of minutes—the time it takes to get online; or they can last for months—the time it takes to build and get involved in an adulterous affair. An important feature of rituals is that it is during this time that we are denying or justifying our sinful behavior. The thought has been birthed in our mind but we haven't carried it out yet—we are just on the way. A question to ask yourself is, "What in your mind makes it okay for you to proceed with the wrong behavior?" Something is happening mentally during the rituals—it could be denial, lying, negotiation, rationalization or rebellion. It is unique to every individual.

Rituals will lead to sexual acting out—it is hard to break the ritual once engaged. Sexual acting out creates more pain, despair and emptiness. Those feelings lead to the enforcement of negative core beliefs, and the whole cycle starts over again.

The goal is to implement a new cycle:

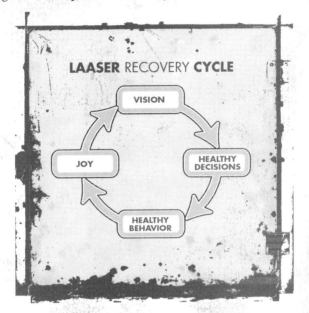

The sexual addiction cycle starts with shame—it starts with those false core beliefs within us. The goal here is to intercept distorted perceptions and replace them with truth. Shower your heart with God's truth about your identity. Bathe yourself in the affirming realities of Scripture. Once you begin to surrender to these beliefs a vision will take form—a new mental outlook for your life. A place you want to be. Instead of the shame-induced fantasy as a means of escape, you can have a joy-directed vision because of God's promised purposes for your life. Fantasy is an imagined outcome of what we would like but that we know will not happen.

Vision is a sense of God working to make us what we were called to be.

Truth leads to vision—if you believe it, you will behold it. Vision leads to healthy decisions—if you see it, you can purpose it. Healthy decisions lead to healthy behaviors—if you purpose it, you will act it. Healthy behaviors lead to joy—if you act it you will experience and believe it. And joy will inevitably lead to more vision! This is the process and cycle of recovery.

PRINCIPLES OF ACCOUNTABILITY-
THE NEHEMIAH STORY

In this section we will use the first six chapters of the book of Nehemiah to discover crucial principles in how to rebuild something that has been lost.

Background. The kingdom of Israel has been overrun and the walls of Jerusalem destroyed during the great Babylonian invasion. Many Jews are in captivity in Persia; others have recently returned to Jerusalem and are no longer exiles. Upon their return, the Israelites experience great distress at the site of their ruined wall. The significance of having a wall that surrounds the city is immeasurable—the structure acts as a vital safeguard against invaders. Some of the Jews send a message to their brother some 600 miles away—in Susa, the Persian capital. His name is Nehemiah and he is cupbearer to King Artaxerxes—a position that may offer hope to the Jews.

Our account starts with Nehemiah hearing the news that the wall has been broken down and the gates have been burned.

CHAPTER 1

"When I heard these things, I sat down and wept. For some days, I mourned and fasted and prayed before the God of heaven." *(verse 4)*

PRINCIPLE ONE: SADNESS

Restoration must start with brokenness. We must come to the place where our sin and our loss brings us great grief. If it does not, there will be no motivation to change. If you are heartbroken, if you are willing to humble yourself before God—then you are ready to start on the path to recovery. "Humble yourselves before the Lord, and he will lift you up." (James 4:10)

PRINCIPLE TWO: CONFESSION

"I confess the sins we Israelites, including myself and my father's house, have committed against you" (verse 6).

We must be willing to take full responsibility for our actions. We must acknowledge our wrongdoings—recognizing that we have brought the consequences upon ourselves—and not seek to blame any other. "If we confess our sins, he is faithful and just and will forgive us our sins and purify us from all unrighteousness." (1 John 1:9)

PRINCIPLE THREE: REPENTANCE

"Remember the instruction you gave your servant Moses, saying, 'If you are unfaithful, I will scatter you among the nations, but if you return to me and obey my commands, then even if your exiled people are at the farthest horizon, I will gather them from there and bring them to the place I have chosen as a dwelling for my Name.'" (verse 9)

Here, Nehemiah reminds God of his promise to gather the Israelites if they return to him and obey. Repentance requires a change of mind and behavior, and results in a realized promise from God. We must be willing to turn from our sin and surrender to Christ in order to reach this new dwelling place of total healing. "There will be more rejoicing in heaven over one sinner who repents than over ninety-nine righteous persons who do not need to repent." (Luke 15:7)

PRINCIPLE FOUR: SUPPLICATION

"Give your servant success." (verse 11)

It is imperative for us to recognize from where our victory will come. It will not be due to all of our efforts, or the efforts of our friends, family or counselor. The source of success is God, and it is to him that we should supplicate. Once you realize that God provides the victory, this principle will become like second nature. "And pray in the Spirit on all occasions with all kinds of prayers and requests." (Ephesians 6:18)

CHAPTER 2

"I was very much afraid, but I said to the king, 'May the king live forever! Why should my face not look sad when the city where my fathers are buried lies in ruins, and its gates have been destroyed by fire?'" (verses 2 & 3)

PRINCIPLE FIVE: HONESTY

The king asked Nehemiah why he looked so sad. No doubt Nehemiah did not want to tell him, but he took a bold step and opened up—and got help because of it. Being honest about our failures is a vital step toward restoration. It often can be a scary step—it is never easy or comfortable to be completely vulnerable—but it will prove to be very rewarding. When we are honest, we give others the chance to help us. "Therefore confess your sins to each other and pray for each other so that you may be healed." (James 5:16)

PRINCIPLE SIX: SUPPORT

"The king had also sent army officers and cavalry with me."
(verse 9)

Nehemiah had only asked the king for letters to the governors providing him safe-conduct on the road. But the king was wise enough to know that Nehemiah would need extra protection along the way, so he sent armed guards to accompany him. In the same way, we will need ample outside support on our journey to freedom. We may be tempted to allow pride to lead us into isolation, but the moment we do, we become vulnerable to destruction. We must stick with a band of people willing to fight for our freedom and well-being. This accountability group must not be one person—it must be a force of many warriors. "Let us not give up meeting together, as some are in the habit of doing, but let us encourage one another—and all the more as you see the Day approaching." (Hebrews 10:25)

PRINCIPLE SEVEN: JUST DO IT

"Let us start rebuilding." *(verse 18)*

Nehemiah told the Jews what he had in mind and they replied by saying, "Let's start!" There was no elaborately laid out plan; there was no detailed instruction. They just decided to show up and begin, ready to trust the Lord and do whatever he required of them. We must not wait until we are in the "right place" to get well. That place does not exist. The work must begin immediately, without delay. Like the disciples of Christ, we must show up ready to follow wherever He leads, not knowing all the places the journey will take us. We can have an idea of the goal, but we will not know all the steps in store for us from bondage to recovery. "In his heart a man plans his course, but the Lord determines his steps." (Proverbs 16:9)

PRINCIPLE EIGHT: EXPECT ADVERSITY

"But when Sanballat the Horonite, Tobiah the Ammonite official and Geshem the Arab heard about it, they mocked and ridiculed us." (verse 19)

Not one of us should be ignorant concerning the enemy's schemes. We must expect adversity on every side—in more than one way. Anytime a person tries to honor God's will, that person must anticipate trouble. Jesus warned us of this fact (John 16:33), the lives of the patriarchs and disciples gave testimony to it (Hebrews 11:36-38), and the epistles attest to it: "So then, those who suffer according to God's will should commit themselves to their faithful Creator and continue to do good." (1 Peter 4:19)

PRINCIPLE NINE:
STAND FIRM ON GOD'S PROMISES

"I answered them by saying, 'The God of heaven will give us success.'" (verse 20)

Nehemiah did not recoil at the first signs of adversity. he fought the attacks with truth and protected his heart from growing faint by demonstrating faith. We are told to use faith as a shield and the Word of God as a sword. (Ephesians 6) When you experience spiritual warfare, you need to remember God's truth and stand firm in faith. Faith is being sure of what we hope for and certain of what we do not see. (Hebrews 11) We should be sure of God's promise to restore and deliver us. "This is the confidence we have in approaching God: that if we ask anything according to his will, he hears us. And if we know that he hears us—whatever we ask—we know that we have what we asked of him." (1 John 5:14)

CHAPTER 3

"Meremoth son of Uriah, the son of Hakkoz, repaired the next section. Next to him Meshullam son of Berekiah, the son of Meshezabel, made repairs, and next to him Zadok son of Baana also made repairs." (verse 4)

PRINCIPLE TEN: DIVIDE THE WORK

Rebuilding the wall in Jerusalem was a huge project—it needed to be divided up into smaller, more manageable tasks. The same is true as we strive for freedom from sexual sin. The healing process can be a giant undertaking. It is imperative that you take it one day at a time. You should divide up the steps so that you are not overwhelmed—even if it means restoration will take longer. "Better a patient man than a warrior." (Proverbs 16:32)

PRINCIPLE ELEVEN:
GET THE GARBAGE OUT OF YOUR LIFE

"Beyond them, Benjamin and Hasshub made repairs in front of their house; and next to them, Azariah son of Maaseiah, the son of Ananiah, made repairs beside his house." (verse 23)

Jerusalem had what was called a Dung Gate. It was the sanitation gate, which was vital or else the city would choke on its own filth. The dung gate channeled all of the garbage out of the city. If you've ever been in a city that was having a garbage strike, you'll understand the importance of the dung gate. What is the filth that you have in your life? What is it you need to get rid of? It could be a stash of pornography, Internet access, cable service, or an affair partner. It is absolutely essential that the garbage be thrown out so that healing can begin.

PRINCIPLE TWELVE:
BUILD CLOSE TO HOME

Each of Nehemiah's workers started with repairs needed around their own homes. Healing for us needs to be similar—each of us should start with restoration of our own home and family. The first year especially should be a time of healing.

CHAPTER FOUR

"…the gaps were being closed." (verse 7)

PRINCIPLE THIRTEEN:
CLOSE WHAT SHOULD NOT BE OPEN

The Israelites worked with all their heart to close the gaps in the wall. We must not approach restoration halfheartedly. Freedom from sexual sin will require a full effort, and part of that means getting rid of any sin at the root. Ask yourself, "What gaps in my life need to be closed up? In what areas am I allowing the enemy to come in? What needs to be eliminated?" It may be that we will need to throw away the television, get rid of access to the Internet, quit our job or cut off any unhealthy relationships. Bottom line is that we must be willing to do whatever it takes to close the gap and shut the door to the enemy. "Put to death, therefore, whatever belongs to your earthly nature." (Colassians 3:5)

PRINCIPLE FOURTEEN:
FORTIFY THE WEAK POINTS

"Therefore I stationed some of the people behind the lowest points of the wall at the exposed places, posting them by families, with their swords, spears and bows." (verse 13)

The enemies of Nehemiah were plotting to attack the people while they were weakest and at a time that they did not expect. Even some of the Jews told Nehemiah with great urgency, "Wherever you turn, they will attack us." (verse 12) His response was to send reinforcements to the places that were most vulnerable. We must prepare in a time of strength for a time of weakness and vulnerability to come. We must not wait to deal with the attack or temptation when it comes, for then it will be too late. Expecting that it will come, and preparing for it in advance is key to victory. We must be in the center of fellowship and accountability every day. This will be our much-needed reinforcement when temptation strikes. "Be self-controlled and alert. Your enemy the devil prowls around like a roaring lion looking for someone to devour." (1 Peter 5:8)

PRINCIPLE FIFTEEN:
FIGHT FOR SOMETHING GREATER THAN YOURSELF

"Remember the Lord, who is great and awesome, and fight for your brothers, your sons and your daughters, your wives and your homes."

Nehemiah knew the men were weary. He assured them of the Great Warrior who would fight for them. Then, he stirred their souls—he reminded them of those who were closest to them. He gave them a reason to fight, a cause to believe in. Often, when we are working toward a self-goal, we can lose focus and motivation fast. But when we expand our vision to include our loved ones, we suddenly have a rising warrior within that wants to protect a great treasure.

PRINCIPLE SIXTEEN: BUILD AND DEFEND

"From that day on, half of my men did the work, while the other half were equipped with spears, shields, bows and armor…Those who carried materials did their work with one hand and held a weapon in the other, and each of the builders wore his sword at his side as he worked." (verses 16-18)

Nehemiah knew the importance of being prepared for attacks while working for the will of God. He had a 50/50 plan—which is also a good system in recovery. While you are working toward victory, it is imperative that you focus equally on defending your good work in the spiritual realm. Nehemiah equipped his men with weapons, shields and armor. This kind of weaponry in the spiritual realm is spelled out for us in Ephesians 6—primarily, the Word of God, prayer and faith. These kinds of practices are crucial as you rebuild your life. Keep the sword at your side! "…With weapons of righteousness in the right hand and in the left..." (2 Corinthians 6:7)

PRINCIPLE SEVENTEEN: GATHER TOGETHER DURING ATTACKS

"Wherever you hear the sound of the trumpet, join us there. Our God will fight for us!" (verse 20).

The sound of a particular trumpet was a battle cry. Men knew to prepare to fight. Nehemiah knew that their fighting would not be nearly as effective unless they gathered in one place. The rebuilding of the wall was an extensive project—the men were spread out all over the place. This principle is key for us. During times of attack, you must gather with other people so that you are not left to face the enemy alone. "Carry each other's burdens, and in this way you will fulfill the law of Christ." (Galations 6:2)

CHAPTER FIVE

"I and my brothers and my men are also lending the people money and grain. But let the exacting of usury stop!" (verse 10)

PRINCIPLE EIGHTEEN:
DO WHATEVER IT TAKES

Nehemiah was willing to sacrifice all he had in order to complete the task God set before him. The Jewish people were experiencing a time of famine and poverty. Nehemiah gave whatever he could to help them. He considered his sacrifice a worthy investment—because his focus remained on the completion of the goal. He did not give up. You may experience a time where all the recovery work begins to take a toll. The process can require a lot of time, money and energy. But God will provide—his grace is sufficient for you. Ask yourself, "What kind of investment am I willing to make in order to see this thing through?"

CHAPTER SIX

"I will not go!" (verse 11)

PRINCIPLE NINETEEN:
DON'T LEAVE THE WORK

Six times, Nehemiah's enemies devised plans to try to lure him away from his work. They had already tried direct attacks and failed; their new scheme was to trick him into leaving the job. Satan will do the same thing. His first attacks will be direct and forceful—trying to get you to give in. But as you stand firm and hold your ground, the enemy will come in more subtle ways. Respond like Nehemiah—with great force. "I will not go!" You must not give up, no matter what messages encourage you to do otherwise. "Let nothing move you. Always give yourselves fully to the work of the Lord, because you know that your labor in the Lord is not in vain." (1 Cor 15:58)

ADDITIONAL **RESOURCES**

The following list of organizations, professionals and advisors (referred to hereafter solely as "advisors") is provided solely for informational purposes. Freedom Begins Here does not endorse and has not undertaken any independent investigation of the qualifications, credentials, experience, education, training, or proper licensing of, any advisor listed below. Freedom Begins Here does not have any direct or indirect input in any advice or services provided by any advisor listed in the book. All descriptive information about advisors has been provided by the advisor directly, and has not been drafted by or certified by Freedom Begins Here.

Any person using contact information provided in this Devotional Journal to locate and select an advisor is strongly encouraged to inquire about the advisor's professional expertise, experience, licensing and qualifications before engaging or hiring such person or organization.

Freedom Begins Here has received no referral fee or other compensation from any advisor listed for the right to be listed herein and receives no referral fee or other compensation based on clientele generated through the following lists.

Freedom Begins Here Counselor Directory

To locate a counselor trained with our accredited curriculum, please visit our website, www.freedombeginshere.org

Organizations:
Faithful and True Ministries
www.faithfulandtrueministries.com
952-746-3882

Smalley Relationship Center
www.smalleyonline.com
800-848-6329

Covenant Eyes
www.covenanteyes.com
877-479-1119

Freedom Everyday: LIFE Ministries
www.freedomeveryday.org
866 408-LIFE

Celebrate Recovery
www.celebraterecovery.com
949-581-0548

Overcomers Outreach
www.overcomersoutreach.com
800-310-3001

Sex Addicts Anonymous
www.saa-recovery.org
800-477-8191

Sex and Love Addicts Anonymous
www.slaafws.org
210-828-7900

Sexaholics Anonymous
www.sa.org
866-424-8777

Bethesda Workshops
www.bethesdaworkshops.org
866-464-HEAL

National Association for Christian Recovery
www.nacronline.com
714-529-6227

Prodigals International
www.iprodigals.com
888-535-5565

National Coalition for the Protection of Children and Families
www.nationalcoalition.org
800-583-2964

Treatment Centers:
Pine Grove Recovery Center
www.pinegrove-treatment.com
888-574-4673

Sierra Tucson
www.sierratucson.com
800-624-5858

The Meadows
www.themeadows.org
800-MEADOWS

KeyStone Center Extended Care Unit
www.keystonecenterecu.net
800-733-6840

National Association of Addiction Treatment Providers
www.naatp.org (Click on "Enter NAATP.org," then click on Members)
717-392-8480

Books:
Healing the Wounds of Sexual Addiction, by Mark Laaser

Out of the Shadows, by Patrick Carnes

The Pornography Trap: Setting Pastor and Laypersons Free from Sexual
Addiction, by Ralph Earle

No Stones: Women Redeemed From Sexual Shame, by Marnie C.
Ferree

For family members:
I Surrender All, by Clay & Renee Crosse

My Husband Has A Secret: Finding Healing for the Betrayal if Sexual
Addiction, by Molly Ann Miller

Rooted in God's Love, by Dale and Juanita Ryan

(To purchase books, go to you local bookstore or favorite online retailer,
such as www.amazon.com.)

Websites/Articles:

Porn Nation
www.pornnation.org/about.htm

CBS News: X-Rated Internet Addiction, Pornography Is As Private As Your Own PC, And Can Become An Obsession
www.cbsnews.com/stories/2007/05/01/eveningnews/eyeontech/main2749789.shtml

Focus on the Family
www.family.org

Interface Institute for Sexual Integrity
www.sexualintegrity.org/mc/page.do

Pornography Statistics
www.blazinggrace.org/pornstatistics.htm

Illusions
www.illusionsprogram.net/index.html

MOTHERS AGAINST PORNOGRAPHY ADDICTION
http://p103.ezboard.com/bmothersagainstpornographyaddiction

Finding freedom from porn addiction, pornography addiction, the effects of pornography
www.everystudent.com/wires/toxic.html

The Alabama Baptist - Pornography and sexual addiction
www.thealabamabaptist.org/ip_template.asp?upid=12447&ctid=2

Abundant Life Ministries - Thrive At Life
www.thriveatlife.org/

For Co-Addicts:

S-Anon International Family Groups (S-Anon)
P.O. Box 111242
Nashville, TN 37222-1242
615-833-3152
www.sanon.org

Codependents of Sex Addicts (COSA)
P.O. Box 14537
Minneapolis, MN 55414
763-537-6904
www.cosa-recovery.org

Al-Anon
Al-Anon Family Group Headquarters, Inc.
1600 Corporate Landing Pkwy.
Virginia Beach, VA 23454-5617
888-425-2666
www.al-anon.org

Codependents Anonymous (CODA)
P.O. Box 33577
Phoenix, AZ 85067-3577
602-277-7991
www.codependents.org

For Couples:
Recovering Couples Anonymous (RCA)
P.O. Box 11029
Oakland, CA
510-663-2312
www.recovering-couples.org

For Trauma Survivors:

Survivors of Incest Anonymous (SIA)
World Service Office
P.O. Box 190
Benson, MD 21018
410-893-3322
www.siawso.org

Incest Survivors Anonymous (ISA)
P.O. Box 17245
Long Beach, CA 90807
562-428-5599

Adult Children of Alcoholics World Service Organization, Inc.
P.O. Box 3216
Torrance, CA 90510
310-534-1815
www.adultchildren.org

NOTES

PersonalToolKit

The Personal Toolkit provides a clear strategy for those struggling with sexual temptation to assess their need, find inspiration for change, and develop a means of personal accountability.

Includes:
- Personal Toolkit DVD
- Exclusive music video to hit song "Undo" by RUSH OF FOOLS
- Devotional Journal
- Covenant Eyes Accountability Software (30-Day Trial)

ChurchToolKit

The Church Toolkit equips churches with the resources needed to recognize and confront pornography and sexual addiction, as well as beginning the journey of recovery for those in need of help.

Includes:
- Leaders Only DVD
- Assessment DVD
- Solutions DVD
- Resource ToolKit CD
- Leader's Resource Guide
- Devotional Journal
- Exclusive music video to hit song "Undo" by RUSH OF FOOLS
- Covenant Eyes Accountability Software (30-Day Trial)

The Smalley Relationship Center provides conferences & resources for couples, singles, parents, and churches. We capture research, connecting to your practical needs & develop new tools for building relationships

resources include:

- Over 50 best-selling books on relationships
- Small Group curriculums on marriage & parenting
- Church-wide campaign series with sermon series, daily emails & more
- Video/DVD series
- Newlywed kit and pre-marital resources

www.garysmalley.com website includes:

- Over 300 articles on practical relationship topics
- Weekly key truths on practical issues
- Daily devotionals
- Conference dates and locations
- Special events
- Free personality & core fear profiles
- Request a SRC Speaker
- **Weekly newsletter:** Receive articles, coaching tips and inspirational encouragement from Gary Smalley which will help you build a more effective and stronger marriage.
- **Profiles:** The overall theme of I Promise is security, and you can take a 20 question test on how secure your most important relationship is. (**Bonus:** After you take that profile consider taking our personality profile which gives you even more insight into what kind of personality styles you and your spouse fall into.)

Visit www.garysmalley.com or call 1.800.848.6329 for Gary's speaking schedule, conferences, and to receive a weekly e-letter with articles.